THE CIVILIZATION OF PERPETUAL MOVEMENT

NICK MCDONELL

The Civilization of Perpetual Movement

Nomads in the Modern World

HURST & COMPANY, LONDON

First published in the United Kingdom in 2016 by
C. Hurst & Co. (Publishers) Ltd.,
41 Great Russell Street, London, WC1B 3PL
© Nick McDonell, 2016
All rights reserved.
Printed in the United Kingdom

Distributed in the United States, Canada and Latin America by
Oxford University Press, 198 Madison Avenue, New York, NY 10016,
United States of America.

The right of Nick McDonell to be identified as the author of
this publication is asserted by him in accordance with the
Copyright, Designs and Patents Act, 1988.

A Cataloguing-in-Publication data record for this book
is available from the British Library.

ISBN: 9781849043984 *hardback*

This book is printed using paper from registered sustainable
and managed sources.

www.hurstpublishers.com

CONTENTS

Preface   vii

1. Nomadism: Its Relation to the International System   1
2. A Short History of Nomad Studies   21
3. Byways Not Controlled: The Securitization of Perpetual
   Mobility   47
4. Economies of Movement   69
5. The Climate of the Commons   91
6. Summation and the Agentic Question   111

Acknowledgments   125
Notes   127
References   147
Index   161

PREFACE

Nomads live all over the world. The last research trip I took was to the arctic. "Chokcha," Isak Triumf told me. The Sami word for autumn. Indigenous to northernmost Europe, many Sami were once nomadic reindeer herders, traveling with the seasons, forever, between Lapland's high tundra and the cold coast of the Norwegian sea. Few live this way anymore, but Isak inherited the practice from his parents and was encouraging his children to carry it on. From his pickup truck, we surveyed a herd. Isak wore snow pants, heavy rubber boots, and a long knife sheathed at his hip. His eyes were bright green, his nose and lips raw from weather and glare.

"Chokatka," I said.

"*Chok*-cha," repeated Isak.

We got out of the truck. Two reindeer carcasses lay, torn and bloody, in the snow.

"Wolverine kill," Isak explained. Poachers hunted in the winter, he continued, but predators hunted all year. Lynx, wolverine, eagle, wolf. He wanted to shoot them, but didn't. In exchange for his restraint, the Norwegian government paid him for animals the predators killed. It was an environmental program, but Isak said it did not work well. The government required documentation. The herders had to search the tundra for carcasses, photograph them, drag them to town. He said he had lost two-hundred-sixty nine animals that year, but received payment for only sixty nine of them.

I couldn't verify this particular claim, but it is the kind of information I have had the pleasure of gathering since I began studying nomadism: the specifics between perpetually mobile people and states. How people are made legible, the environmental implications, security regulations:

"*Chok*-cha," repeated Isak.

"Chohakcha," I tried again. "Chuckchuka."

By that trip I was accustomed to mangling languages and inspecting livestock. When I began research for this book, though, I didn't know about nomads in the arctic, or anything about nomadism at all, really. I didn't even know I was on a research trip. But everything I heard about nomads struck me as interesting. Like this:

"This man is a nomad, he doesn't get lost."

It was a joke, told by English anthropologist Alex de Waal, about Tuareg linguist Ibrahim ag Youssef. We three were riding in a minivan, in circles, around al-Fasher, Sudan. It was 2007 and Alex and Ibrahim had been recruited as advisors to the Darfur peace process. I was reporting a magazine story, which, that afternoon, entailed staring out the window at the low dry town and hoping we would get shot at in such a way that no one was injured. I was a foolish twenty three years old. We were lost.

Beside me in the backseat, Ibrahim tugged at his grey beard and occasionally narrated the scenery. He was wry and generous in his observations, which were not particularly useful for my magazine piece but did, in part, lead to this book. Our talk ranged widely, from horses to French literature to Sufism to photography. Ibrahim's most striking habit in conversation was to sniff the edge of his head scarf, as though it were a fragrant bloom, a peony perhaps. One afternoon I asked him about this, and he offered me a whiff. Before he'd left Mali, Ibrahim explained as I inhaled, he had distilled the urine of his favorite female camel and soaked the end of his scarf in the brew. He found the odor comforting when homesick. I'm not sure now if he was kidding or not. Over those weeks he had several jokes. But when, one day, I asked him if he was joking about being a nomad, he said, very seriously: absolutely not.

It was around then I became actively interested in nomadism, and not only because of Ibrahim (who appears again, later in this book). In those weeks he and Alex met with several compelling groups of nomads. Some were reasonable, some were responsible for the worst crimes of the war in Darfur, but dialogue with all of them was integral to peace. So we introduced ourselves beside their Hiluxes, lunched in the acacias' shade, listened to complaints about land tenure, drought, and the UN. It was my first experience of armed conflict and nomadism was an important element, just as, I'd learn much later, it was an important element of arctic wildlife conservation.

PREFACE

Nomadism is one of humanity's great shared practices. It is how we all lived, once, and though obscured and diminished it remains vital. Still, for all the interesting nomads and nomad scholars I've met, most people, if they think of nomadism, think it is finished, or irrelevant. They think of gypsies, perhaps, or Lawrence of Arabia. They do not think of Isak, or Ibrahim, Leica round his neck, arguing that nomadism is critical to understanding conflict across Africa. But it is. In fact, it is useful to understanding a multitude of problems around the world. Nomadism has much to give to modern international relations and political theory. This is what *The Civilization of Perpetual Movement* aims to prove.

Not everyone will agree. Which, in fact, is why I wrote the book. In graduate school I was assigned a text—quoted at length in the following pages—which argues that nomadism has played "no major role in world history for the past five hundred years." This is completely incorrect. I know because after that Sudan trip, wherever I worked as a reporter, I asked about nomads, and interviewed them if I could. Though frequently sad, the research was always worth the trouble, and relevant to whatever I was covering.

My excellent publisher, Mr. Michael Dwyer, has suggested that I explain here how I got the "nomad bug." I hope what I have written to this point does so, a bit, but for now I'll leave the topic. Unfortunately, nomadism attracts more than its share of wacky self-obsession, and so I'm reluctant to go much further into my own story, what got me to Sudan in the first place and carried me on to central Asia, the Arctic, and elsewhere. Indeed, the rest of the book, as I hope you will see, aspires to *anti* travel literature, an impersonal register, in an attempt to bring the topic of nomadism inside the traditionally formal discipline of international relations.

That written: if, like me, you are a compulsive reader of introductions and conclusions, a skimmer of bodies and skeptic of academia and textbooks, I none the less ask you give even the middle of this book your attention, in the hope that, as many nomads will tell you, the journey is equal to the destination.

Nick McDonell   Khartoum and New York,
                                                                    Autumn 2015

1

NOMADISM

ITS RELATION TO THE INTERNATIONAL SYSTEM

There is no consensus on the definition of nomadism. Competing definitions are functions of the underlying assumptions and priorities of their authors. Some definitions indicate that nomadism does not belong in the study of international relations (IR). By dealing with the topic at all, this book adopts certain stances about the discipline of IR as well as about nomadism. These stances come out of the critical tradition.

The element of that tradition which has immediate bearing on a definition of nomadism is a commitment to interdisciplinarity. As the sociologist Justin Rosenberg writes, "the way the disciplines divide up social reality itself involves taking as natural (and therefore overlooking) certain basic things about the modern world which to both Smith and Marx seemed novel and needful of explanation…"[1] This book does not presume to break ground like those two thinkers. It does, however, seek to address the status quo critically rather than solve[2] a problem. Currently, the international relations status quo excludes nomadism:

> Although attempts have been made to accommodate units as different as city-states and agrarian empires within established theories of IR, little, if any, effort has been made to take account of nomadic tribes. The lack of interest is perhaps unsurprising because these units have had no major role in world history for the past five hundred years.[3]

This is from the theorists Buzan and Little, and can be said to represent the field. What follows attempts to revise this view by asking the following question: how do nomadism and the international system relate? The essential answer is that nomadism is a form of political expression that influences international security, trade, and conservation processes.

To make this large, central argument, we will first seek a workable definition of the term nomadism. The common understanding is too broad, often cloudy, and unreflective: people who move around a lot, shepherds. The more technical definitions of the term are contentious—at least, within a certain, mostly anthropological, community. None of the current definitions, common or technical, are quite adequate for a study of the international system which is dedicated to clarity and committed to inter-disciplinary communication.

A new definition, however, will provide a starting point for thinking about the relationship between nomadism and IR in four areas: i) sophisticated state-centrism as articulated by Stephen Krasner; ii) mainstream conceptions of property based on the work of John Locke; iii) the emergent indigenous peoples' rights regime; and iv) international law and nomadism as articulated in Jérémie Gilbert's 2007 article proposing a *nomadic lex specialis*.

These discussions will contextualize subsequent analysis in chapters devoted to a history of the field (2), security (3), trade (4), and climate change (5) respectively. The concluding chapter (6) provides a summation, areas for further study, recurring problems in the field, and addresses directly the question of nomadic agency. The book engages mostly with populations in Sudan, Kenya, Afghanistan, Mongolia, China and Mali. It could, however, have relied on sources from Australia, the US, Europe, the Middle East, and other African countries. Source availability played a role in selection—but not at the expense of conceptual consistency. Cases were chosen based on their relevance to all three of the book's prisms: security, trade, and climate change. If a population appears in one section, it can bear comparable analysis in another. Thus chapter 5 analyzes Tibetan nomads in China in terms of the climate change regime, but those nomads could have appeared in chapter 3, in security analysis; and so on. This transitivity lends heft and generalizability to the definition. It also suggests that while Tuareg are analyzed rather than the Polisario, the Janjaweed rather than the Nunavut, it could have been otherwise.

For all these populations, nomadic history is largely unwritten. As James Scott puts it: "it is the peasant's job to stay out of the archives,"[4] and the same is true of nomads. Written nomadic sources do exist—from

Sami newspapers to Bedouin novels—and the book draws on them when possible. But such sources are rare. The topic must be approached obliquely, or by interviews. Understanding this, the book draws on a wide range of often conflicting sources, including: news reports; legal documents; government cables;[5] author observations and interviews (usually interpreted) from Sudan, Kenya, Ethiopia, Afghanistan, Mongolia, and Norway between 2007 and 2015; and scholarly works quantitative and qualitative. All relevant methods of analysis and their sometimes conflicting rationales for case selection—from rangeland ecology to close reading (or "discourse analysis")—enrich the overarching attempt to understand patterns in the relationship between nomadism and the international system.

A New Definition of Nomadism

But what is nomadism? The first instance of the word in English is dated to 1587, but the etymology goes back to classical Latin—nomad, nomas, meaning "member of a wandering pastoral tribe"—and ancient Greek: "νομαδ" meaning "pasturage," followed by a suffix. When it deals with nomadism at all, literature on the international system tends to engage unreflectively with the layperson's definition of the term—the *Oxford English Dictionary*'s, for example:

> nomad, *n.*
>
> A member of a people that travels from place to place to find fresh pasture for its animals, and has no permanent home. Also (in extended use): an itinerant person; a wanderer. Cf. nomade *n. rare* before 19th cent.[6]

As Gilbert, Philip Carl Salzman,[7] and others have pointed out, this definition is based on the *motivation* for movement: keeping animals alive. The definition[8] does not account for or imagine other motivations. Common parlance thus suggests food production, an economic interpretation. Anthropologists have likewise tended to break nomadism down into (highly developed) categories and define it based on production: nomadic pastoralists, nomadic hunter-gatherers, and nomadic service providers. There is a wealth of research on each, and a host of other sub-groups. But the most common development in the literature, and the starting point for a new definition, is the opening idea of Humphrey and Sneath's book *The End of Nomadism?* "The very category of nomadism," they write, "has ceased to be analytically useful."[9]

3

Others[10] have been moving in this direction for decades, but none make the point quite so forcefully. Sneath and Humphrey do so in support of their argument that "far from being a practice associated with the most backwards herders, highly mobile livestock herding is often the basis for the most efficient...production, and that it is compatible with technologically advanced and profit oriented economic activity." To show this, their book contrasts twentieth-century mobile herding in Russia, China, and Mongolia. They are right. It is a powerful argument against economic justifications for sedentarization[11] and in defense of mobility as an economic tool. Theirs is an ambitious project, given the long history of perceived "backwardness" of mobile herders. And given this project, it is understandable that Sneath and Humphrey should like to banish the word "nomad" from the discourse—contrary to this book, which would refer to some of their "mobile herders" as such. As they point out, "nomad" is a highly loaded term. Among other characteristics, it can connote egalitarianism, barbarity or unreason. To escape these associations, they define nomadism as a fluid "economic practice"—"a series of local knowledges and techniques located in particular historical circumstances."[12]

But this definition demarcates the political and the economic in a way with which others have rightly taken issue. As Rosenberg asserts:

> We need to step outside the existing disciplines and think as the earlier social theorists did in terms of the social world as a whole—as a social totality. We have to do this because it turns out that the disciplinary division of labour between the modern social sciences itself reflects uncritically and thereby naturalizes the distinctive social forms of modernity.[13]

By isolating nomadism as an economic practice, Sneath and Humphrey naturalize certain ideas. The separation reinforces a dominant neo-liberal discourse that, as Roger Tooze argues, "sets out a specific and special relationship between politics and economics in which the rationality of economics should generally triumph over the irrationality of politics."[14] Put another way, calling nomadism an economic practice de-politicizes it.

Sneath and Humphrey also argue that the term "nomadism" should be abandoned because it "is a category imagined by outsiders." This claim is supported by their own interviews in central Asia. But it surely is overpowered, or at least complicated, by competing research in the same region and elsewhere,[15] recent Bedouin historiography,[16] and international agreements[17] composed by nomads, to name only three counter-examples. There are clearly people who refer to themselves as nomads, though the definition might remain unclear or even mistaken. Sometimes, as we shall see when we look at nomad-specific non-governmental organizations (NGOs), these people capitalize on the associations and conceptual muddle that Sneath and Humphrey are trying to eliminate. But the word itself is a tool that nomadic populations have at their disposal. This is not to call Sneath and Humphrey's argument unsophisticated. It is excellent. They discuss the aesthetic and cultural contributions of nomadism to the societies they study. They often question the inherited situation—for example, discussing the construction of markets for pastoral products rather than their "natural" emergence. And they are highly sensitive to the political implications of their findings. In fact, they often critically analyze relations between states and nomads. In light of all this, their rejection of the term represents a missed opportunity, rather than a failure of understanding.

Some of their contemporaries are closer to seizing that opportunity. Like Sneath and Humphrey, however, almost all have rejected the term "nomadism" in favor of "mobility." Mobility has become the dominant term to the degree that the first international agreement about nomadism, in 2002, was named the Dana Declaration on Mobile Peoples and Conservation. As defined by its authors:

> By mobile peoples, we mean a subset of indigenous and traditional peoples whose livelihoods depend on extensive common property use of natural resources over an area, who use mobility as a management strategy for dealing with sustainable use and conservation, and who possess a distinctive cultural identity and natural resource management system.[18]

The declaration was signed by twenty-seven "concerned professionals, including social and natural scientists from all regions of the world" after a conference in the Wadi Dana Nature reserve in Jordan in April, 2002. To Sneath and Humphrey's definition, this introduces elements of indigenous peoples and conservation theory. Still, the definition depoliticizes mobility by calling it a "management strategy" and focusing on its relation to sustainable development and conservation. This was the intent of some of the Declaration's authors. According to Dawn Chatty, who helped write the document, "what we wanted was a document that a nation could sign on to. It was a compromise document."[19]

We shall explore the historical circumstances of the Declaration's emergence in greater detail later. For the sake of building a definition however, we can simply note here that it engages in de-politicization; that it rejects the associative power of the word "nomad;" that it is concerned as much with conservation as nomadism; and that it was born a "compromise document." Like Sneath and Humphrey's definition, the Dana definition is in wide use, and a useful starting point, albeit not ideal for work dedicated to holistic political understanding.

A few members of the Dana Committee went on to work on a new document, *The Segovia Declaration of Nomadic and Transhumant Pastoralists*, in 2007. As is clear from the title, this group reclaimed the term "nomadism." But their preamble is based around a description of "migratory pastoralism" that is very similar to the Dana Declaration. Moreover, they use the terms "migratory pastoralism," "transhumance," "nomadism," and "mobility" interchangeably. Sometimes people are "mobile and nomadic;" at other times "nomadic and transhumant." Though the document implies elements of this book's definition of nomadism, it suffers from a lack of clarity and never defines the term.

The only other international document of note which particularly addresses nomads is the 1991 International Labour Organization (ILO) Convention 169:

> Article 14: The rights of ownership and possession of the peoples concerned over the lands which they traditionally occupy shall be recognised....Particular attention shall be paid to the situation of nomadic peoples and shifting cultivators in this respect.[20]

ILO 169 is the "Indigenous and Tribal Peoples Convention," hence we can infer that it defines nomadic peoples as indigenous. Beyond that, however, there is no definition. This is not sufficient for the peoples in question. The definition of "indigenous" itself remains debated, and under certain definitions, particularly emerging from Asian and African states,[21] there are nomadic populations that would not qualify. "Nomadic" is also a much older concept than "indigenous." It would be incoherent, and ironic, to subsume it totally in indigenous peoples theory—which is based on chronology.

Given then that these latest definitions are both unsatisfactory, how should we define nomadism?

Definition is important. Language is inherently relational, and if one accepts certain strands of the post-structural and critical traditions, inextricable from power. A word like "nomadic" is more than a descriptor—it sets up a binary opposition (nomadic/sedentary) and governs the boundaries of discourse on the topic. Ultimately it delineates a community, which is itself a problematic term. But constructive discussion requires definitions, not just an awareness of mutability. And so rather than reject ideas that are so clearly central to human experience on the basis of ambiguities, we should, as Ken Booth argues, "recognize that in working through [their] potentialities and problems we are in fact helping to constitute a different kind of world politics." To that different (more "multi-dimensional and inclusive") end, he defines an "emancipatory community" as:

> a free association of individuals, recognizing their solidarity in relation to common conceptions of what it is to live an ethical life…an emancipatory community will recognize that people have multiple identities, that a person's identity can not be defined by one attribution, and that people must be allowed simultaneously to live in a variety of communities.[22]

In this context, nomads are a community, and nomadism is the practice of perpetual mobility as a form of political expression essential to cultural identity and livelihood.

While most definitions, like those we have touched on, depoliticize nomads by emphasizing a mode of economic production; or Dana-esque conservation; or, in earlier periods, a "primitive" stage of cultural development; this definition does several things. i) It reflects the history of nomadic relations to rather than dependency on the state (in its juxtaposition of identity and "political[23] expression"); ii) it engages with "social totality" by collapsing the political, cultural, and economic; it is easily identifiable ("perpetual mobility" = no intention of permanent settlement, even divided between multiple sites); iii) and finally it strives for inclusivity.[24] Nor does it exclude the economic, conservationist, or other views that have enriched nomad studies. Rather, it emphasizes nomad-state relations and brings the topic into the field of international relations.

The immediate problem with such a definition, it could be argued, is that it is too broad. Who determines what is "essential"? If someone says she is nomadic, then does she fit our definition? No definition is perfect, but the discussion each generates can be constructive. The aforementioned questions serve this definition's key motivation, namely to demonstrate that nomadism is overlooked as a political practice. *Why* does that someone have no permanent abode? Though the definition affords some space for nomadism among self-identifying "global citizens" of the transnational elite—a highly mobile population with inordinate control over the political discourse—it also legitimizes the phenomena as a political choice for a majority that is disenfranchised by that discourse. It is an irony, which echoes Frederick Barth's famous notion that sedentarization happens only to the richest and poorest Basseri nomads of Iran, that contemporary nomadism tends to be the province of the world's very richest and very poorest inhabitants. Both groups employ it as a means of state evasion.

Little surprise, then, that state representatives have often tried to set their own definitions. To take one of the many[25] examples: in the anglophone world, the term "semi-nomad" was likely coined[26] by Lieutenant General Sir John Bagot Glubb during his time in the Middle East in the 1920s. But what began in his military[27] manual entered the anthropological vocabulary. The problematic consequences of adding "semi" to "nomad" would be familiar to post-colonial thinkers and are clear to Chatty, who argues that the definition represents

> typologies based on movement (e.g., fully-nomadic, semi-nomadic, semi-settled) [that] were used to break down the organization of the Bedouin and to confirm ideas of modernization theory that settled existence was far superior to a mobile one.[28]

Such definitions remain in use around the world, and their implicit arguments continue to characterize debates over nomadism and state policy. There were explicit repercussions for such terms too. Chatty notes that in this instance, in Syria, nomads and "semi-nomads" fell under the jurisdiction of separate courts. For his part, Glubb limited "true" Bedouin nomads to "certain specified tribes"[29]—presumably specified by himself, and thus subject to a court of his choice.

In this light we should reject utilitarian definitions like Glubb's not only because they lack sound theoretical justification, but because they exemplify arbitrary state dominance of nomadic populations. Our definition, by contrast, comes from a tradition of scholarship on the state-subject relationship and on nomadism, from thinkers like Frederick Barth, Pierre Clastres, Owen Lattimore, Ernest Gellner, and James C. Scott. All of these scholars present evidence that nomadism is not simply a livelihood, a stage of socio-economic development, or a cultural inheritance, but, per our definition, a political choice. The most recent and radical of them is Scott, whose book, *The Art of Not Being Governed*, provides crucial background for our new definition.

He introduces that volume as an "anarchist history of upland Southeast Asia" which he sees ultimately as a "fragment of what might be properly considered a global history of populations trying to avoid, or having been extruded by, the state." Though Scott does not define it, he identifies nomadism as one of the strategies of state-evasion of the populations he is describing. He concludes of his proposed global anarchist history that "such a task is clearly beyond me and, ideally, it would be a collaborative undertaking by a great many scholars."

The following chapters of this book can be read as an attempt to pursue the collaboration Scott hopes for, but without focus on a particular geographic area. Instead, it focuses on nomadism itself—which is not itself "anarchist," but is a practice critical to Scott's proposed history. And it does so in the contemporary period.

Scott warns that his analysis "makes little sense for the period following the Second World War." The reasons he offers, echoing Lattimore's analysis in the 1930s, run as follows.

> Since 1945, and in some cases before then, the power of the state to deploy distance demolishing technologies…so changed the strategic balance of power between self-governing peoples and nation-states, so diminished the friction of the terrain, that my analysis largely ceases to be useful. On the contrary, the sovereign nation-state is now busy projecting its power to its outermost territorial boundaries and mopping up zones of weak or no sovereignty. The need for natural resources of the 'tribal zone' and the desire to ensure the security and productivity of the periphery has led, everywhere, to strategies of 'engulfment,' in which presumptively loyal and land hungry valley populations are transplanted to the hills. So if my analysis does not apply to late-twentieth-century Southeast Asia, don't say I didn't warn you.[30]

This is an accurate assessment. The zones of "weak or no sovereignty" he chronicles are shrinking. But this does not mean that the practices— like nomadism—of the relevant populations are no longer employed. They are, and to ignore them is to accept uncritically the "engulfment" he mentions. The objective here is not to decry that engulfment—a futile effort if ever there was one (as Scott writes, "about the long-run trend there can not be a shred of doubt"). The aim, rather, is to draw attention to it, to question it. Scott's 1945 cutoff is also, he admits, informed by his particular interest in Southeast Asia. Scholars of other regions insist on the continued relevance, and occasional primacy, of anarchist populations in their region's "peripheral" zones—the Syrian Desert,[31] for example, and areas of Western Sudan.[32]

9

Moving beyond this period-of-analysis caveat, there are several ways in which Scott's work is key to understanding nomadism as we have defined it. Of the several principles of state evasion he identifies in Southeast Asia, the second...

> ...is mobility: the ability to change location. The inaccessibility of a society is amplified if, in addition to being located at the periphery of power, it can easily shift to a more remote and advantageous site. Just as there is a gradient of remoteness from state centers, so also we might imagine a gradient of mobility from a relatively frictionless ability to shift location to a relative immobility. The classic example of physical mobility is, of course, pastoral nomadism.[33]

It is an important point for this work's definition that the "classic" example is pastoral nomadism—it is not the *only* example. This is especially relevant in the context of the Dana Declaration, because of the debates[34] some of its authors had over the potential pastoral domination of international nomadic representation. Scott does not privilege the pastoralists. He identifies mobility as a practice of state evasion for foragers, the so-called sea gypsies, hunter-gatherers, and swidden agriculturalists, among other groups. No current definition of nomadism accounts for all of these, however. On the contrary, as we saw among the anthropologists, thinkers have been trying to narrow the definition. But if "nomadism" is to have conceptual power in terms of the state, interstate system and international relations discourse, it must move in the *opposite* direction, and emphasize shared practice despite the variety of its forms.[35] Orang Laut sailing along the Indonesian coast are obviously different from the steppe Yomuts Scott describes to make some of his points. But the principle, as defined here, is sufficiently powerful that one could replace Yomut with Orang Laut; flocks of sheep with schools of fish; Persia with Johore, and still maintain the integrity of the following passage.

> Moving with their flocks and herds...such nomads are constrained by their need for pasture but are unmatched in their ability to move quickly over large distances. Their mobility is at the same time admirably suited to the raiding of states and of sedentary peoples....for our purposes, however, what is important are the evasive strategies vis-à-vis state power that nomadism makes possible. Thus, for example, Yomut Turkmen, located on the periphery of Persian state power, have used their nomadic mobility to raid grain growing communities and escape taxes and conscription of the Persian Authorities.[36]

For all nomads then, Scott here provides a historical framework. Numerous defining reactions of the state follow and can be quantified:

re-direction of the military, concentration of the tax code, potential rationing.

Nomadism and Some Theories and Assumptions in International Relations

In a recent review, Stephen Krasner discussed the deeper, less obvious implications of Scott's work, and by extension our definition.

> James C. Scott is the un-Hobbes. He does not simply celebrate the virtues of what we generally regard as primitive societies; he rejects the conventional wisdom that these societies are primitive at all, seeing them, rather, as a reaction against and superior to states, at least most states for most of human history.[37]

Perhaps unintentionally, Krasner highlights one of the reasons nomadism, grounded in Scott's work, is such a useful concept for building on the critical tradition. That is: it identifies a significant population (a subsection of Krasner's "primitive societies") who, by definition, challenge a variety of the ontological and methodological assumptions on which mainstream international relations is based.

The most obvious of these assumptions is state-centrism. This "units"[38] question is what drives Buzan and Little's argument that nomads "have had no major role in world history for the past five hundred years." Buzan is neither extremely dogmatic nor conservative. In the 1980s he was integral in the expansion of security studies' traditional military focus to the areas of political, economic, societal, and ecological security. But as Steve Smith and others have pointed out, he has always insisted on the state as the prime referent. His dismissive attitude towards nomads is consistent with—and emblematic of—statist frameworks, even if highly sophisticated.

Those frameworks might seem, at first glance, to capture nomadism effectively. Krasner's four-fold definition of sovereignty—domestic, interdependence, international legal, and Westphalian—is quite good at accounting for behavior by populations, like nomads, whose behavior might otherwise undermine the accepted dominance, benefits, flexibility, or inevitability of the state system. Consider for example the Rizegat of Northern Darfur crossing the Sudan-Chad border.[39] Such action violates interdependence sovereignty, which is distinguished by the successful regulation of borders. As Krasner demonstrates, this has happened repeatedly throughout history, and often without impact on domestic sovereignty. To make this point, he relies on the distinction between authority and control,[40] and applies it not only for domestic sovereignty, but for the international legal and Westphalian varieties. And while interdependence sovereignty, i.e. border control, might be violated, other key elements of state sovereignty are not. Even though Sudanese and Chadian governments cannot regulate their borders, they can still arrest citizens, Kenya still recognizes them as states, and The Hague still sees them as units subject to international law. According to Krasner, implications follow for globalization and non-state actors: "it is nowhere near as self-evident as many observers have suggested that the international environment at the end of the twentieth century has reached unprecedented levels of openness that are placing new and unique strains on states."[41] Or, read another way—the state rightly remains the prime referent.

But there is more to nomadism, and the other practices of state-evasion, than an aversion to borders. Elsewhere in his review of Scott, Krasner identifies one of the central problems raised by *The Art of Not Being Governed*, and ideally our definition. The "our" he deploys here fairly stands in for mainstream international relations of the Buzan and Little variety.

> It is not easy to fit Scott's discussion into our contemporary understanding of state development, which has been dominated by three theoretical approaches: modernization theory, institutional capacity, and rational choice institutionalism. Despite their great differences...all are premised on the assumption that effective governance—governance by a state or some other institutional structure with geographic reach, and scope over some range of activities (beginning with taxation and war)—is, if not good in some absolute sense, better than life without a state.

This clarifies what he meant by calling Scott the "un-Hobbes"—that Scott prefers "life without a state" to "effective governance." But it is not a convincing argument. It hinges upon an idea that Krasner does not make explicitly: that the communities Scott describes—including nomadic communities—do not actually have "effective governance."

They do. Krasner's ideas of "governance" (security and taxes, at a minimum) are not necessarily theirs. In fact, his ideas of effective governance—the traditional state-making projects—are often antithetical to nomadism and exist to prevent it. As Scott writes, "sedentarization is just about the oldest state project in the world...the obvious fact that a sedentary population is easier to count, tax, conscript, and survey than a fugitive population is only the beginning of the story."[42]

For some critical thinkers in international relations, it is easy to make room for Scott's discussion in "our contemporary understanding of state development." The first way they do so is by questioning the primacy of the state in our thinking. Andrew Linklater suggests that critical theory begins

> with the Kantian proposition that everything hinges on how political community is constructed, particularly in the most powerful regions. From this vantage point, it is a profound mistake to ignore the respects in which states threaten their own citizens so that the study of international relations is free to develop its specific focus on the ways in which states interact with and threaten each other. ...Consequently, critical theory does not begin with how independent political communities conduct their external relations but with the deeper question of how they are constituted in the first place.[43]

Everywhere it exists, nomadism is part of the answer to that deeper question. We will be looking specifically at the ways it contributes to that constitution in later sections: in nomadic aversion to borders, stewardship of natural resources, military potential, and inherent trade networks, among other contributions. But the question at hand is how nomadism challenges state-centrism at a more theoretical level. Krasner's review is telling again. "Scott's discussion makes it clear that it was, and still is, more desirable to live in the hills of Burma than under the oppression of the Burmese state," he writes, "but Copenhagen, London, and New York, perhaps even New Haven, would be more attractive to most people."

The in-joke about New Haven—where Scott is director of the Agrarian Studies Program at Yale—is not malicious, but it suggests an elitism that characterizes Krasner's presumption about what "most people" want. Most nomads, presented the choice between living in the desert and living in a mansion (even in Palo Alto), might take the mansion. But they are not offered such a choice. Typically, states present them with much less attractive options, if it offers them at all. Most often the state simply attempts sedentarization. The question for Krasner, and state-centrism, is this: why should nomads (or other "primitive societies") not be allowed to remain nomads? Krasner's answer to this question is again based on why "most people" would rather live in Copenhagen.

> The impediments to improvements in basic human well-being—longer life expectancy, lower child mortality, less illness—are now political, not material. Most of the citizens of open-access societies enjoy physical security and material prosperity. On average, they live longer than men or women have ever

lived before. Rarely do their children die before the age of five. Bearing a child does not carry the threat of death. Scott's pessimism may yet be warranted. We could blow ourselves up. But other paths are also open. There is more wisdom in Hobbes, or at least Locke, than Scott allows.[44]

This Lockean-Hobbesian defense of the state emphasizes monetary prosperity and security over aesthetic, cultural, and spiritual elements of nomadism that are sometimes incompatible with sedentarization. It also wrongly assumes nomadism and technological modernity are incompatible. But it does, reasonably, summon a universal human desire for security, long life, and health evident in Locke. It turns out, however, that Locke's work on property in the *Second Treatise of Government* is based on some assumptions that do not make sense from a nomadic perspective either. And these sedentary assumptions have no inherent value greater than the nomadic alternatives which could have been, and in many cases already do, exist.

It is not surprising that the ideas of a seventeenth-century intellectual born in Somerset did not make sense for nomads—a category of people widely perceived, at the time, to be savage or even sub-human. In examining the foundations of the system Locke helped to articulate, however, this book tries to do more than contribute to the continuing challenge to Eurocentrism in a historical sociological[45] sense. The point is not to problematize for its own sake, nor even to deny states' prominence in the global system. It is rather to present a view of that system—parts of it at least—which suggests a reevaluation of the way its institutions should deal with nomads.

Nomadism and Property Beyond the Human Rights Discourse

Jérémie Gilbert, in his essay "Nomadic Territories: A Human Rights Approach to Nomadic People's Land Rights," has already begun that reevaluation from a legal point of view. He traces the precedents of sedentary victory in law to the "agricultural argument" of the eighteenth century. Locke was a key proponent of this idea, which derived from his quest to articulate "a means *to appropriate* [lands] in some way or other before they can be of any use, or at all beneficial to any particular man."

The idea is that cultivation and/or successful resource extraction are the basis for title to property.[46] It also is manifest in the work of Rousseau, Kant, and Vattel. Gilbert locates it in a series of eighteenth- and nineteenth-century legal arguments concerning the dispossession of Amerindians in the North American colonies and concludes that, as a result of this theory of "effective occupation," "nomadic peoples have been regarded as legally non-existent."[47]

Gilbert does not examine why Locke and these thinkers make the agricultural argument. Rather, he makes a case for its injustice in the context of the human rights discourse. But if we look critically—nomadically—at the foundations of Locke's thinking about property, we can deal with the agricultural argument in another way, on the terms set by its proponents—whose heirs dominate the policy world today.

Locke argues that God has given the earth to "mankind in common" to take "their best advantage of Life, and convenience." There is a corollary to this in his point that "nothing was made by God for Man to spoil or destroy."[48] This is more powerful than a simply "religious" argument. If we have the flexibility of mind to replace God with a secular humanism (a path many have reasoned out), it becomes easy to identify with Locke's motivation for making the agricultural argument, even for an athiest: greater production to improve the lot of Man—alleviate hunger, for example.

Studies in recent decades—like Humphrey and Sneath's work—indicate that nomadism is often the most productive use of the land through which nomads pass.[49] Nomadism has also been shown repeatedly to do less damage to the environment than agriculture, not to mention the major extractive initiatives that often replace it as a means of economic production.[50] Much of the world's nomadic population lives in regions that are not fit for cultivation at all. It was the particularly bad luck of American Indians to occupy the fertile ground which figures so centrally in the legal arguments Gilbert traces. If productive use of property is the basis for territorial delineation, in many regions Locke might now concede that "Mankinde" would be better served by nomadism's use of land than by agriculture alone.

There are contemporary thinkers who take this argument to a radical conclusion. The anthropologist and political theorist Jared Diamond contends that agriculture was "the worst mistake in the history of the human race," the origin of "the gross social and sexual inequality, the disease and despotism, that curse our existence."[51] That is an extreme reaction, but most states, international laws, and theorists like Krasner do not ever question the sedentary-agricultural origins of property.

Nomadism and Indigenous People's Rights[52]

Gilbert is searching for the most effective way of fighting consequent attitudes. This is why, beyond arguing that the international legal system does injustice to nomads, one of his key goals is to "evaluate the role of human rights law in ensuring nomadic people's access to and use of their traditional transhumant territories."[53] To do this, he not only touches on the agricultural argument—whose foundations we have just considered—but the principle of *terra nullius*: the idea "that any uninhabited territory is open to conquest and can be occupied by states." "It was only in 1992," he points out, "that the fiction of 'empty land' (*terra nullius*) was recognized as discriminatory and racist in essence." The landmark case was tried in Australia; later cases were fought in Canada and elsewhere.[54]

Gilbert finds that the cases most beneficial to nomadic populations tend to rely on elements of the evolving discourse on indigenous rights in their decisions. At their most effective, some even recognize property ownership based on "traditional" or "customary" indigenous land use. No cases, however, recognize the possibility of sovereignty. On the basis of this tendency, Gilbert concludes:

> ...overall, under the banner of indigenous people's [IP] rights, nomadic peoples have gained some recognitions of their rights to land...This has to be seen as the best path for nomadic peoples' future, as it marks a recognition that they do have a right to be different and that such a right entails their right to maintain their own perspective on the interaction between a people and a territory.[55]

Gilbert is right, but it is important to consider why the situation "has to be seen" this way. The argument raises a theoretical tension between Scott and Gilbert that is straightforward but intractable. If nomadism, as Scott has it, is an essentially anti-state political expression, integrating it into an essentially statist UN, IP or conservation project is difficult.

Our definition builds on Scott's ideas about anarchist populations to try to solve this problem. For Scott, mobility is a means of state evasion—but nomadism is not always anti-state. There are numerous examples, historical and contemporary, of self-interested collaboration between nomads and sedentary states, from the Orang Laut with the Sultanate of Johore in the seventeenth century to the Janjaweed with the current government of Sudan. The use of statist human rights and indigenous people's law by an emergent, internationally conscious group of nomads and their allies—like

Gilbert—is an evolution of nomadic exploitation of state concepts and structures. The exploitation has become international and abstract. The increasing spatial control over nomads at the state level, exercised by virtue of technology, has in recent decades had an inverse relation to the increase in stated nomadic rights at the international level. In a few instances—Afghanistan, Tanzania, for the Roma in Europe—the discourse around these rights has had direct consequences for state-nomad relations in national law and development.

But the tension remains. Recognition of collaborative nomad-inter-state behavior alleviates but does not resolve it. Despite the aforementioned counter-examples, nomadism is typically a means of state evasion. The cost to states of the integration of nomadism into an international framework remains an open question of which Gilbert is aware. One answer implicit in his analysis is that the current state system, partly based on Locke's sedentarist conception of property, is so deeply entrenched that it is impossible to make significant gains for nomads beyond the emergent theoretical regime.[56] In this scenario the reality of nomadism is too threatening; if nomads were to announce themselves as willfully evading the state, they would receive even less sympathetic attention than they do, and probably more negative.

But we should not take that state of affairs—or potential nomadic announcements—for granted. Historical explanations for the de-legitimization and unpopularity of certain transnational movements are identifiable. Nomadism could have come to greater prominence via the "Spirit of Bandung," the pan-African-Asian movement which emerged from the eponymous conference in 1955. But, though actively promoting non-state consciousness, it was dominated by sedentary projects.[57] The flow and current ebb of this tendency is not neatly explicable. It is tied to the rise and fall of men like Nehru and Nasser; the influence of the Cold War on newly independent African and Asian states; the end of the Bretton Woods system and re-calibration of international financial institutions like the IMF; the failure of the "New International Economic Order"; and other factors besides. Had events progressed differently, a much stronger trans-national push by the Indigenous Peoples (IP) community in the run up to the UN adoption of the Declaration on the Rights of Indigenous Peoples (UNDRIP) might have taken place. Nomadism might have been mentioned, at least. It would seem a small concession to anti-state behavior when, less than fifty years prior, thinkers in the Non-alignment movement were legitimizing even the use of violence—see, for example, the Geneva Convention on the rights of national liberation movements.[58]

But this is not the atmosphere in which Gilbert is writing today. His argument that indigenous people's legal theory represents the best means forward for nomadic peoples is well supported with his case material. He concludes, and this book concurs, that indigenous people's rights are not sufficient for dealing with nomadism under international law. Gilbert offers four reasons for this, beyond some of those already discussed: i) indigenous people's rights are legally under-developed; ii) the definition of "indigenous" is still being debated, and under certain definitions some nomadic communities would not qualify; iii) indigenous people's rights remains controversial in some regions, and so a designation as indigenous might be harmful to some nomadic communities; and finally iv) the present body of law regarding indigenous peoples does not address nomads directly.

For these reasons, Gilbert proposes a "*Nomadic Lex Specialis,*" beyond indigenous people's law, which would allow nomads to respond to increasing pressure and perpetuate their way of life. The key areas of this *lex specialis* would be usufructuary rights, like hunting and grazing, and rights relating to what he calls an "enlarged approach to freedom of movement."

Developing this strategy sidesteps another theoretical problem facing both Scott's work on resistance and this book. Edward Said articulates it succinctly:

> …Although Scott presents a brilliant empirical as well as theoretical account of everyday resistances to hegemony, he too undercuts the very resistance he admires and respects by in a sense revealing the secrets of its strength.[59]

This problem of 'undercutting' is manifest not only in theoretical arguments, but also in the activities of some of the INGOs dealing with nomadism, e.g. the relationship between the Tanzanian state, the tourist industry, and nomadic peoples in the Serengeti.

Gilbert's development of international law is essentially foreign to nomadic traditions of state evasion/exploitation. It is rather an additional strategy, born of a sedentarist legal tradition. It is highly unusual in its explicit engagement with nomadism on the international stage, and will remain a key contribution in the field. The corpus of law it identifies may, finally, be one of the few tools nomadic populations have at their disposal to perpetuate their way of life in a political-theoretical environment where, as Stephen Krasner concludes in his review of Scott's book:

The shadow of Hobbes's Leviathan, and for that matter of Locke's Second Treatise and Rousseau's Social Contract, has set the boundaries concerning how we think about, and value, political authority.[60]

Nomadism has enjoyed scant recognition as political practice within those boundaries—but, as the next chapter demonstrates, there is a rich line of thought that suggests it always should have.

2

A SHORT HISTORY OF NOMAD STUDIES

There are few histories of nomad studies,[1] and none concerned with nomads in the international system. The most widely read is probably the introduction to A.M. Khazanov's *Nomads and the Outside World*. That work, published in 1984, is a comparative anthropological look at particularly pastoral nomadism. It begins by asserting the great length of time for which writers have been considering nomads—"the myth of the nomad may be even older than the myth of the 'noble savage.'"[2] This is an extremely common assertion in nomad studies, and writers often make it more forcefully: "nomads have been the subject of attention from Western writers for a very long time indeed..."[3]

This attention to the age of the discipline is consistent across a spectrum of conceptual frameworks. At one end, scholars actively encase nomads in a philosophical system about what constitutes the good life and society. At the other, scholars analyze nomads without explicitly advocating a larger philosophical project. The first current dominates from Antiquity through the middle of twentieth century; the latter has swelled since then. Theories of modernization characterize the first; competing theories of anthropological inquiry characterize the second. Crucially, the two currents are not mutually exclusive.

The following history will follow both through a series of key sources in the field, including Khazanov. All continue to affect perceptions of nomadism by nomads, and by others. They do so directly—when scholars and practitioners consult them—but also through the myths they

21

have contributed to, or helped to undermine. Close reading will help to explain under what conditions the contemporary idea of nomadism in the international system emerged; contextualize this book's definition of the term; and show how foundational texts undermine or support common myths of nomadism. Most importantly, it will illustrate a tradition of engagement with nomadism as a political practice and expression. This book emerged from that tradition, and this history will explore it in Antiquity; the Middle Ages; the Enlightenment and nineteenth century; the early and mid-twentieth century; and the late twentieth century and present day.

Antiquity and the Bible

In 1860, the French Egyptologist Auguste Mariette uncovered a hieroglyph-covered limestone slab near Abydos, on the banks of the Nile. Later archeologists dated it to the middle of the third millennium BCE, and eventually translated it. *The Autobiography of Weni*[4] remains much cited, both as an example of our species' earliest writings and as a historical document of the time. Weni was a government official and eventually general under three pharaohs.[5] If his slab is to be believed, he was famous for his military exploits. Most notable among them: relentless pursuit of "sand-dwellers."[6]

Scholars of the period believe this evocative phrase refers to nomads ranging from today's central Egypt to Sinai and the Levant.[7] Weni doesn't go into great hieroglyphic detail, but his reference reminds us that since there has been writing, there has been writing about nomadism—and its political implications. Weni himself reports going to war with the "sand-dwellers" on five separate occasions, and there is reference to them in a variety of the period's texts.

Weni's preeminent translator, James Beard, suggests that the "sand-dwellers" might have been the Caananites,[8] and their namesake is one of history's most famous nomads. His debut in the Book of Genesis illustrates the complexity of the nomad archetype in ancient sources.

> 2: And Abel was a keeper of sheep, but Cain was a tiller of the ground. 3: And in process of time it came to pass, that Cain brought of the fruit of the ground an offering unto the LORD. 4: And Abel, he also brought of the firstlings of his flock and of the fat thereof. And the LORD had respect unto Abel and to his offering: 5: But unto Cain and to his offering he had not respect.[9]

In the conventional myth of the nomad, the herder is backwards, and the farmer is civilized—closer to God, one might say here. But if God's approval is any measure, here the herder is more civilized. At least, herder and farmer in Genesis begin on equal footing.

And Cain was very wroth, and his countenance fell....

8: And Cain talked with Abel his brother: and it came to pass, when they were in the field, that Cain rose up against Abel his brother, and slew him. 9: And the LORD said unto Cain, Where is Abel thy brother? And he said, I know not: Am I my brother's keeper?

This contravenes another widely received myth: the violent nomad. Here is original murder, but committed by a farmer against a herder. Of course, we might ask if Abel is really a nomad at this point. Not all herders are nomads, though pastoralism implies mobility. This issue was to become very important in the definitional arguments that began in the late twentieth century. The myth of the nomad, however, is impossible to dissociate from herders—mobile or not. To the present day, some explanations of conflict remain rooted in an idea of inherent tension between pastoralist and agriculturalist. The conflict in Darfur is the most vibrant recent example. There, as elsewhere, the dominant narrative is one in which herders attack farmers. That, however, is not what happened in Genesis.

10: And he said, What hast thou done? the voice of thy brother's blood crieth unto me from the ground. 11: And now art thou cursed from the earth, which hath opened her mouth to receive thy brother's blood from thy hand; 12: When thou tillest the ground, it shall not henceforth yield unto thee her strength; a fugitive and a vagabond shalt thou be in the earth. 13: And Cain said unto the LORD, My punishment is greater than I can bear.[10]

Another common myth, which continues to have repercussions, is that nomadism precedes agriculture. We shall explore this point later. Here we should note simply that, again, the myth we are familiar with is not borne out in the text. Cain was a farmer before he began to wander. Once Cain becomes a nomad, of course, many of the familiar elements of the myth are clear in the story. That wandering is a curse; that nomads are incapable of agriculture; that they are criminal and violent; that they do not want to be nomads; that they are selfish, not their brother's keeper; and so forth

But who was the nomad, Cain or Abel? Both could bear the label: the pastoralist, and the wanderer. Nomad and farmer are not linked just because they are brothers—they are linked because both could be nomads. All of this is to say: even in the foundational documents, the myths were never simple. When they seemed so, as later critical theories will rightly argue, they were being put to particular political use.

Herodotus

Herodotus, the fifth-century BCE Greek scholar, would have agreed. It is a boon that the first major secular account of a nomadic population comes to us from his *Histories* of the Greco-Persian wars of the period—including Darius I's conquest of Egypt. The "father of history" is silent on the fate of the "sand-dwellers," but has much to say about the nomadic Scythians of Eurasia whom Darius encountered.

In Herdotus' account, the most powerful Scythians practise no agriculture and live in wagons. "War and plunder," Herodotus writes, "are the source of this people's livelihood."[11] They are thus unable to govern. During the period of their dominance in Asia "violence and neglect of law led to absolute chaos."[12] Likewise they are ungovernable: "the mere suggestion of slavery filled the Scythian chieftains with rage." Considerable and fantastic details proceed from these observations. "Scythian custom is for every man to drink the blood of the first man he kills….Many Scythians sew scalps together and make cloaks out of them."[13] Sometimes Herodotus connects nomadism to cruelty, without clear explanation: "the reason why they blind their prisoners of war is connected with the fact that the Scythians are not an agricultural people, but nomadic."[14]

In their blood-thirst, Scythian nomads are the ur-barbarians. Their presentation in this foundational document helps explain why nomads came to be imagined as they are. However, Herodotus comments upon some behaviors in the *Histories* that suggest they were not as categorically exotic in his view as in later perception. "It is not their custom to make statues,"[15] but they worship Zeus, and they have kings. Moreover, Herodotus presents anecdotes that reveal that nomadism was political practice of a kind, though radically different from his own people's. He records, for example, their attempt at a census.

> [In Exampeus[16]] there stands a brazen bowl….this huge vessel was made of arrowheads; for one of their kings, named Ariantes, wishing to know how many men there were in Scythia, gave orders that each of them should bring him a single arrowhead, failure to do so being punishable by death. An enor-

mous number were brought, and Ariantes decided to turn them into something which might serve as a permanent record. The result was the Brazen bowl....[17]

Herodotus estimates the bowl to hold five hundred gallons. More interesting than its size is the lack of information and control it highlights, from a Greek City-state perspective—"considering" as Herodotus notes, "the power and importance of Scythia." Elsewhere in his account, Scythian leaders pass incognito as Greeks, confederate and parlay. In these senses they are a legitimate political force, even while drinking blood.

They do not, however, conform to the counting, taxing, conscripting and other state-control practices of the Greek city-states. Instead, they have the brazen bowl—and their own notion of the good life. In one remarkable passage, Herodotus reports on an exchange between Darius and the Scythian leader, Idanthyrsus. The Scythians have been moving constantly, to the frustration of the Persians. "'Why on earth, strange man,' the message ran, 'do you keep running away?'"

"'Persian,' Idanthyrsus replied, 'I have never yet run from any man in fear; and I am not doing so now from you. There is, for me, nothing unusual in what I have been doing: it is precisely the sort of life I always lead, even in times of peace...'"[18]

The exchange highlights one of the great misconceptions about nomads: that they wouldn't move if they didn't have to. Idanthyrsus' full-throated rebuttal of Darius' loaded question is rare (for the time) and clear: nomadism is a choice. Whether Herodotus recognizes the agency or not, the value of nomadism is not totally lost on him. "The Scythians," he concludes, "though in other respects I do not admire them, have managed one thing, and that the most important thing in human affairs, better than anyone else on the face of the earth: I mean their own preservation. For such is their manner of life that no one who invades their country...can come to grips with them."[19]

Herodotus was wrong, of course. The Scythians, like Weni's "sand-dwellers," would eventually be conquered or driven to the fringes of empire. The written body of justification and understanding of that process, of which Herodotus was a founder, would grow ever larger in parallel. Herodotus, like many scholars after him, was sometimes sympathetic to nomads and even noted aspects of their perpetual movement which were willful, political, and equal to the sedentary. But no such observation would seriously compete with barbarism as the governing understanding for two millennia. Mostly, from Herodotus and Weni onwards, nomad studies were written by people at war with nomads.

Records of the Grand Historian

The preeminent scholar of nomads in the ancient Eastern tradition, Chinese Historian Ssu-Ma-Chi'en, fit the pattern. He penned the vast *Shiji*, better known as the Records of The Grand Historian, under the patronage of Emperor Wu, at the turn of the first century BCE. Wu's reign saw the greatest imperial expansion of the Han Dynasty, and was marked by decades of battle with the nomads of the Central Asian steppe. These battles brought very bad fortune to Ssu-Ma-Chi'en. As a punishment for his support of one of Wu's generals—ignominiously defeated by those nomads—the historian was castrated. He continued work on his histories as palace eunuch, and it is in this context that he devoted a chapter to the nomadic Xiongnu. He is surprisingly sympathetic to them—but then, they were not the ones who castrated him. Though Ssu-ma-Chi'en calls nomads barbarians, the word is misleading, and his descriptions of their traditions imply political agency. Absent are the animal similes prevalent in Western scholarship, ancient and beyond.

In fact, not only for his own time but in his account of previous centuries, the Grand Historian often equates the Chinese and the Xiongnu. According to his translator, Watson:

> The ancestors of the Chou dynasty lived for generations among the western barbarians while as late as the end of the Spring and Autumn period (481 B.C.) we read of Duke Chuang of the state of Wei who could look down from his castle tower upon a barbarian settlement in the midst of his territory. We are often reminded that the people of the state of Ch'in were half barbarian in their ways, while the state of Ch'u frankly admitted that its ancestors were barbarians.[20]

It is possible that, like Tacitus' commentary on the Germans, Ssu-Ma-Chi'en's modest admiration for the "barbarians" is ironic. "Their laws are simple and easy to carry out, the relations between ruler and subject is relaxed and intimate, so that the governing of the whole nation is no more complicated than the governing of one person." More than most, the Grand Historian would have known that no nation can be governed as a single person. He also notes that the Xiongnu are unlettered and know "nothing of propriety or righteousness.

And yet there are moments in his text where he compares the Xiongnu favorably with his own people in earnest. He notes, for example, that they never imprison a criminal for more than ten days in the process of deciding his punishment. This must be, in part, because they lack prisons—but according to Watson, it also invites "comparison with the situation in China...when the jails were full to overflowing with men awaiting sentence." "The number of imprisoned men for the whole barbarian nation," writes the Grand Historian, "does not exceed [a] handful."[21]

It is also notable that Ssu-ma-Chi'en refers to the Xiongnu as a "nation," though they "have no walled cities or fixed dwellings....or any kind of agriculture." As Lattimore would note millennia later, this was a very rich time for nomadic-sedentary political relations. Ssu-ma-Chi'en establishes the common stereotypes—blood-thirst, horsemanship, avarice—but he also reports on nomadic political wisdom. The relevant passage, in which a Han envoy reports back from parlay with the Xiongnu, recalls Herodotus' account of Idanthyrsus' response to Darius. "All the multitudes of the Xiongnu nation would not amount to one province in the Han Empire. The strength of the Xiongnu lies in the very fact that their food and clothing are different from those of the Chinese, and they are therefore not dependent on the Han for anything." The envoy goes on to point out that Han silks are no good for riding through the wilderness, and that the Xiongnu would be foolish to adopt them as more than treasure. The envoy has disdain for the ignorance of his own court on the topic: "just because you wear hats, what does that make you?"

Today, one argument for the relocation of the nomads is that, as a mobile people, they are not closely connected to their traditional lands. This fallacy is commonly exploited by resource extraction advocates the world over—but especially in the Gobi desert. It is an historical irony that Ssu-ma-Chi'en repudiates this misconception in a story concerning the same region, millennia before the current controversy (which we shall explore in chapter 5).

In his anecdote, a Xiongnu leader named Mo-tun has ascended to power and is visited by an envoy from another group of nomads, "to ask if they could have [his father's] famous horse that could run a thousand *li* in one day." Against the advice of his ministers, Mo-Tun sends the horse. "'When a neighboring country asks for it,'" he explains, "'why should I begrudge them one horse.'" He repeats himself when they ask for his favorite concubine. The punchline comes when they ask for the most desolate part of the Gobi desert—a place so barren it is worth less than a horse, or a mistress. At this request, Mo-tun "flew into a rage." ""Land is the basis of the nation!"" he said. 'why should I give it away?' And he executed all the ministers who had advised him to do so."[22]

Without over-reaching, we can note that the current argument between radical nomad conservationists and the Mongolian government follows a similar path. Nomad conservationists argue that licensing parts of the desert to extractive industry robs them of their identity. The government points out that the potential income is equivalent to more than thirty percent of the country's current GDP. Which is not to say that Ssu-Ma-Chi'en would align himself with nomad conservationists. He would likely, however, have recorded some of their voices, as he did in his own time. Like Herodotus, he was more nuanced, open-minded, and thorough than many scholars of nomadism to follow. After the Middle Ages, encounters between nomads and sedentary populations became less and less equal. The combination of centralized government, population density, and technology carried the trend into the present.

But not before nomads invaded the center of Western civilization.

Ammianus Marcellinus

Ammianus Marcellinus saw it coming. He was a soldier before he was a historian, of the Roman Empire in late decline. His accounts of emperors Constantius to Valens are given to digression—making him perhaps less practical in his own field than Tacitus or Livy, but more useful to nomad studies. He devotes a section of book 31 of *The Later Roman Empire* to "the nature of the Huns and Alans."

"None of them ploughs or ever touches a plough handle," he writes. "They have no fixed abode, no home or law or settled manner of life, but wander like refugees...No one if asked can tell where he comes from, having been conceived in one place, born somewhere else, and raised even further off." Like Herodotus before him, Marcellinus foregrounds nomadism in gore—"their most coveted trophy is to use the flayed skins of their decapitated foes as trappings for their horses"[23]—and there is no reasoned connection between barbarity and mobility. As his translators note, *The Later Roman Empire* is much influenced by literary stereotypes and fantasy: "his nomads, Huns or Saracens, bear an uncanny generic similarity, while the notion that the Huns half cooked their meat by placing it under their saddles is a typical piece of learned invention."[24] The hoofs of Herodotus' Scythian beasts resound on each page—as indeed some were beating to Rome in Marcellinus's lifetime.

Perhaps this is why, of the various historians here considered, Marcellinus dehumanizes them most. "The enemy and their crazy leaders were as dangerous as so many wild beasts."[25] Animal similes remain prevalent throughout his account. But, as opposed to various Roman precursors—Pliny the Elder described the nomadic Blemmyae "as being without heads, their mouths eyes attached to their chest"[26]—Marcellinus concedes nomadic "shape, however disagreeable" is human, even if nomads are "totally ignorant of the distinction between right and wrong."

And the relentless "otherization" of nomads is also tempered by observations of behavior in line with Marcellinus's own politics. Rather than join the imperial bureaucracy—the common mode of advancement for young aristocrats—he took the unusual step of joining the army, and the military background informs his work. In this context, his observation that the Eurasian nomads "choose as their leaders men who have proved their worth by long experience in war"[27] stands out—especially in contrast to the poor Roman strategists whose failures he documents. "They are not subject to the authority of any king," he continues, "but break through any obstacle in their path under the improvised command of their chief men." Marcellinus was righter than he would live to know. Nineteen years after his death, Alaric and his Visigoths sacked Rome, fulfilling the ultimate sedentary fear of the nomadic.

The Koran

At the southern and eastern edges of that collapsing empire, Islamic civilization was rising—and defining its own relations to nomadism. These were also, mostly, antagonistic. In the Koran's initial characterization of nomadic Bedouin, in Sura at-Tawbah, or "the Repentance," they are "more stubborn in unbelief" than other non-believers. The explanations and consequence of their godlessness resonate with today's stereotypical nomad attributes. Firstly they are lazy—those who "rejoiced in tarrying behind the Messenger of God, and were averse to struggle with their possessions and their selves."[28] Worse, they are seen to be liars: "they say with their tongues what is not in their hearts"—or at least dissemblers:

"the Bedouins came with their excuses...."[29] Life in their world is a grim, heathen fate, akin to punishment: the confederated invaders of Medina would "wish that they were desert dwellers among the Bedouin"[30] should they attack again. In the majority of the Suras they simply remain savages in that desert—"a people corrupt."[31]

But they are not without their uses. In Sura forty-two ("The Muhammadat") they are called upon to fight—not in the sense of *jihad* prescribed for believers elsewhere, but in exchange for "a goodly wage." This early example of nomad as mercenary is a powerful idea that recurs throughout the history of thought on the topic—and not without reason, as we shall see in our chapter on nomadism and security. The relation cannot be understood totally as a payoff—this "wage" comes from Allah as well—but the sense of Bedouin interaction with higher authority of any kind is decidedly mercantile.

It is also impious. The Bedouin twice offer excuses for their late belief on account of worldly concerns: "'We were occupied by our possessions and our families, so ask forgiveness for us.'"[32] This too resonates with later conceptions. Certain nomads, particularly the Roma population, are (in)famous for their concern with the acquisition of goods, and the Bedouin are early painted so. There is even a sense of pity in this misconception, condescension to the nomad who is so careful of such meager belongings. Later notions (consider T.E. Lawrence's cinema-famous line about the "clean" desert) paint the nomad ascetic, free of cumbersome city goods. But in the period of the Koran's compilation, Bedouin were perhaps too dangerous for such romanticization.

But neither were they static. The Bedouin of Sura forty-nine eventually convert. They do so incorrectly—aggressively, individually—but they do so all the same. The Book attempts to correct them this way: "the Bedouins say, 'We believe.' Say: 'You do not believe; rather say 'we surrender...'"[33] What the Bedouins say might be more attractive to anyone not given to political or religious submission, but the Koran is inescapable literature. That the Bedouins are conceivable inside the fold, however imperfectly, creates space for their greater political significance in the work of Muslim thinkers on the topic.

Ibn Khaldun

The most influential of these must be Ibn Khaldun (1332–1406), who is often regarded as the father of nomad studies. Ibn Khaldun was a scholar and diplomat famous for, among other exploits, supposedly climbing down the citadel walls of Damascus to meet the conqueror Tamerlane in 1401. His magnum opus is the *Muqaddimah*, a work of world history and universal philosophy sometimes credited with introducing the scientific method to social phenomena. It is perhaps most commonly remembered for a cyclical theory of state formation in which "tribes well up out of arid regions to take over cities where in turn they lose their collective solidarity."[34]

In the process of articulating this theory, Ibn Khaldun pays particular attention to the nomadic Bedouin. The full chapter he devotes, his clear prose (in translation), and his nuanced thinking must all account for the frequency with which scholars of nomadism refer to him. From the outset, he defines the Bedouins by their mobility, which in turn is defined opposite civilization. "All the customary activities of the Bedouin lead to wandering and movement. This is the antithesis and negation of stationariness, which produces civilization..."[35]

Ibn Khaldun provided explanations for why this was the case. Some were crude: "as compared with sedentary people, they are on a level with wild, untamable animals and dumb beasts of prey."[36] Other explanations were more complex: "Bedouins are not concerned with laws...under the rule of Bedouins, their subjects live in a state of anarchy...." At one point, Ibn Khaldun even discusses the Bedouin's relations to labor to explain their backwardness:

> ...since they use force to make craftsmen and professional workers do their work, they do not see any value in it and do not pay them for it. Now, labour is the real basis of profit, when labour is not appreciated and is done for nothing, the hope for profit vanishes, and no productive work is done. The sedentary population disperses, and civilization decays.[37]

This prefigures arguments over whether nomads are "feudalist" or "anti-feudalist" which we shall see in the twentieth-century Soviet debates. But it is most important as introduction to the following argument, which persists today: "Bedouins, thus, are the basis of, and prior to, cities and sedentary people....urbanization is found to be the goal to which the Bedouin aspires."[38]

Chronologically, this has been disproven. The archaeological record indicates that the most famous type of nomadism—nomadic pastoralism—postdates agriculture.[39] Ibn Khaldun had no fossil isotope analysis with which to ascertain this. Would that he had—the notion that nomadism is prior to sedentarism on an ascent towards civilization has been astonishingly hardy.

Ibn Khaldun's ideas about nomads, however, were not strictly teleological. His conception of society is cyclical, and his observations suggest a symbiotic relationship: "while [the Bedouins] need cities for their necessities of life, the urban population needs [the Bedouins] for conveniences and luxuries...." Perhaps most famously, Ibn Khaldun wrote that the desert—metonymically, nomadism—was the "reservoir" of civilization. The constitutive relationship of this metaphor foreshadows a key element of continental philosophy and critical theory in international relations. Nomads are prototypical "Others." In this reading, civilization needs the Bedouin—Ibn Khaldun never suggests that it could fully conquer them. Indeed, he wrote that "when there is no militia, or when the dynasty is weak.... [the city's] inhabitants succumb utterly to the Bedouins and....their civilization is wiped out."[40]

At the other end of the cycle, though, Ibn Khaldun observes that "when there is a ruler in a city, the submissiveness and obedience of the Bedouins is the result of the [city] ruler's superiority." He continues in a vein that simultaneously calls to mind both Machiavelli and the current situation of many nomadic populations.

> ...a leader makes [the Bedouins] obey him and exert themselves in behalf of his interests...even if he has to cause some discord among them so as to get the support of one party, with the help of which he will then be able to overcome the remainder and thus force the others to obey him... [These Bedouins] often can not leave particular districts [and go] to other regions, because all of them are [already] inhabited by other Bedouins who usurped them and kept others out of them.[41]

In this, we can read both an articulation of indirect rule and the political consequences of sedentarization. We should not make too much of these resonances, of course. Ibn Khaldun was not a critical theorist. But he did seem to recognize that ruler and ruled, "civilized" and "savage," were connected in ways that were not altogether obvious. He saw this particularly in nomadism. Meeting Tamerlane at the gates of Damascus would no doubt impress upon one the importance of the practice.

The Anthropology of the Enlightenment and Nineteenth Century

Ibn Khaldun's emphasis on nomadism on the path to state formation was an influential idea. It was particularly useful to Enlightenment era proto-anthropologists. The eighteenth-century French writer and politician C.F. Volney, for example, concluded of nomads he observed in Syria that "as often as the different wandering tribes find peace and security, and a possibility of securing sufficient provisions, in any district, they take up their residence in it and adopt...a settled life and the arts of cultivation...."[42] Several of the great thinkers of Volney's time shared this notion, with slight variation. Kant, for one, wrote that the banding together of men to "protect their property from tribes of pastoral Nomads...meant that certain steps were taken to establish a civil constitution and the public administration of justice." He described, in these "crude beginnings,"[43] the origins of culture, civil security, inequality, freedom, despotism, and much else. Likewise, Adam Smith, more narrowly, described nomadic society as a stage of economic development.[44] Progress was the order of the day.

But nomadism did not sit easily as a cipher in a schematic of human development. It was at the time a consequential political phenomenon. Ibn Khaldun's ideas about nomadism did not survive by chance, or oral tradition—they were translated and put to work. In the nineteenth century, in fact, it was the French Ministry of War which published several chapters of the *Muqaddimah* concerning Berber history as an *Histoire des Berbères*. The results were, perhaps, predictable. Abdelmajid Hannoum argues that:

> The *Histoire des Berbères*...has become since then the source of French knowledge of North Africa. It is upon that French narrative that colonial and postcolonial historians have constructed their knowledge of North Africa, of Arabs, and of Berbers....The writing of Ibn Khaldûn was translated and transformed in the process in such a way as to become a French narrative with colonial categories specific to the nineteenth century.[45]

Such behavior did not originate with European colonialists. Ibn Khaldun, in the original, was pursuing the Arabization of the Berbers, some of whom were nomads, and some not. But the *Histoire Des Berbères* discarded unmanageable, cyclical, constitutive elements of nomadic Berber history and emphasized a teleological progress that was more in line with French interests.[46]

Our man Volney did not leave the Middle East with an entirely teleological view, however. We can even read in his writing evidence of Scott's theories of state evasion: "when...the tyranny of government drives the inhabitants of village to extremity, the peasants desert their houses, withdraw with their families into the mountains, or wander in the

plains, taking care frequently to change their place of habitation...."
This clearly casts mobility as a political choice—centuries ahead of Scott
and other critical anthropologists—even if Volney concludes with the
assertion that the "cultivating state is that to which mankind is most natu-
rally inclined."[47]

Such was the consensus of his time. And by the second half of the
nineteenth century, many Europeans, like Volney, had some first hand
experience with nomads. But prominent late twentieth-century scholars
of nomadism, like Khazanov and Neville Dyson-Hudson, would call the
works of this period "not very skilled"[48] and "sloppy."[49] Dyson-Hudson
went on to lament that "nomadic studies ha[s] a curiously inchoate,
non-cumulative character." Particularly in this period, he claimed that:

> ...the complex interaction of scholarly speculation and direct observation
> which did so much for the early growth of anthropology simply never devel-
> oped as far as pastoral nomads were concerned. Orientalist, geographical, and
> anthropological impulses remained separate, and such knowledge as there was
> became scattered across three largely self-insulating fields of inquiry.[50]

Dyson-Hudson's complaint is really one about missing the big picture.
It zeroes in on a pattern recurring throughout the literature of the
Enlightenment and nineteenth century. That is: authors dismiss or fail to
recognize the political importance of nomadic groups, but their attention
inadvertently builds a case for exactly that.

W. Robertson Smith's work[51] on nomadic tribes in Arabia is a good
final nineteenth-century example. Echoing Ibn Khaldun, he writes
that: "[their] life supplied the type on which all Arabian society was
mainly moulded." He also points out that nomadism is not random,
"not to be thought of as roaming quite at large through the length and
breadth of the peninsula." He even discusses nomads in a political
vernacular: "among nomadic Arabs we find that a certain number of
groups might form a confederation presenting the semblance of something like a nation...."[52]

And yet he doesn't, quite, make the political jump—he sees only "the
semblance" of the political. This fits contemporaneous myths of sav-
agery, i.e. the vast and unchanging difference between "a wild Bedouin
and a rich merchant of Mecca." It is easy to identify with Dyson-
Hudson's frustration while reading Robertson Smith's explanation for
why nomads do not have politics, as such. It is clearly a political argument: indeed, it resembles arguments in international relations, for,

among other phenomena, the limited capacity of international institutions: "the tendency of each group to stand by its own members in every quarrel [is] fatal to the permanence of such unions."[53]

The Recognition of Political Nomadism in the Twentieth Century

In the next period, some thinkers made the jump that Robertson Smith never did. They began to articulate the political implications of their observations. The majority did not, however. The topic remained dominated by anthropology, and according to both Dyson-Hudson and Khazanov, the beginning of the twentieth century saw a widening of the gap between anthropological theory and nomadic studies. They particularly refer to the slow adoption of Malinowskian attitudes by European[54] anthropologists studying nomads, and conclude that the "watershed" in anthropology did not come until the 1950s.

There were several dramatic exceptions. The most famous not only discussed the political implications of nomadism, but participated in them. T.E. Lawrence is sometimes overwhelmed with admiration for the Bedouin, and at other moments compares them to beasts with the same vehemence as Ammianus Marcellinus. His opus, *Seven Pillars of Wisdom*, is both full of contradictions and necessary to an understanding of the muddled romance surrounding nomad studies. A key problem is the sedentary scholar's desire to become a politically active nomad himself. "Pray God," Lawrence writes, with his usual drama, "that men reading this story will not, for love of the glamour of strangeness, go out to prostitute themselves and their talents in serving another race."[55] In his dealings with the Bedouins, of course, he believes he is doing exactly that. At the very end of his book, Lawrence provides the following explanation.

> The strongest motive throughout had been a personal one, not mentioned here, but present to me, I think, every hour of these two years. Active pains and joys might fling up, like towers, among my days: but, refluent as air, this hidden urge re-formed, to be the persisting element of life, till near the end. It was dead, before we reached Damascus.

There are a few other reasons. His "pugnacious wish to win the war"; curiosity; historical ambition of "hustling into form, while I lived, the new Asia which time was inexorably bringing upon us." He became very famous for doing just that, an icon of the twentieth century. The movie depicting his adventures among the Arabian Bedouin is one of the touchstones of cinema, and contributed mightily to Lawrence's argument that "Bedouin ways were hard even for those brought up to them, and for strangers terrible: a death in life. When the march or labour ended," he writes, "I had no energy to record sensation."[56]

Still, he was prolific—and from his many ethnographic observations he ultimately inferred a "master type" of nomad in the form of his friend and ally Auda.

> His hospitality was sweeping; except to very hungry souls, inconvenient. His generosity kept him always poor, despite the profits of a hundred raids. He had married twenty-eight times, had been wounded thirteen times; whilst the battles he provoked had seen all his tribesmen hurt and most of his relations killed. He himself had slain seventy-five men, Arabs, with his own hand in battle: and never a man except in battle. Of the number of dead Turks he could give no account: they did not enter the register....he saw life as a saga. All events in it were significant: all personages in contact with him heroic.[57]

Lawrence's accounts of his own adventures are as fabulous and suspect as his description of Auda. Biographers have long since disproven several sleepless desert crossings (he had a snooze or two). In fact, contemporary reviewers realized that they were dealing, largely, with fiction. After reducing *Seven Pillars* to a paragraph of its essential elements—attacks on the railway, Akaba, the fall of Damascus—E.M. Forster concluded: "That is what the book is about, and it could only be reviewed by a staff officer who knows about the East. That is what the book is about, and *Moby Dick* was about catching a whale."[58] The recognition of invention in Lawrence's work, however, did not prevent him from becoming an archetype as intimately bound up with nomadism as Chingis Khan. Rather it did the opposite.

In contrast, the exceptional scholarly works on nomadism of the period never became as well known. Indeed, even the seminal works—by Owen Lattimore and E.E. Evans-Pritchard—are located in other fields. As Dyson-Hudson notes of the latter: "his achievement was perceived in the context of African anthropology (cattle cultures) and the field of social structure (lineage systems) rather than as the first modern study of problems central to nomadism."[59] Similarly, Lattimore is remembered as a historian of China, rather than a theorist of nomadic studies. Both thinkers, however, should also be read as pioneers in that field, who insisted on the explicitly political nature of nomadism.

Evans-Pritchard makes the point throughout his famous study of the Nuer, conducted in the 1930s. "Political institutions are its main theme," he writes in his introduction, and it is the good fortune of nomadic studies that such a major work of social anthropology alighted on a mobile population. Like his nineteenth-century predecessors, Evans-Pritchard's work was "undertaken at the request of, and was mainly financed by" a government, in his case, that of the Anglo-Egyptian Sudan. Unlike his predecessors, however, he was a professional anthropologist, interested foremost in study (though a decade later he would put his knowledge of Sudan to use, leading Anuak irregulars against Italian forces in World War II). His immersion in Nuer society seemed near total—to the degree that he became "hardened, though never entirely insensitive, to performing the most intimate operations in full view of the camp."[60] This kind of immersive research ultimately led him to the methodological assertion for which he remains famous—that anthropology was not science at all, but history. In this light, mobility, like other elements of Nuer society, was a choice rather than a "natural state."

Evans-Pritchard was aware of the step he was taking. "In the way we have written this book we have in some measure broken away from the tradition of lengthy monographs on primitive peoples," he writes. "We have also tried to describe Nuer social organization on a more abstract plane than is usual." In this way he legitimates Nuer society in relation to the traditional sedentary state, though it remains very different. Evans-Pritchard notes, for example, "the lines of political cleavage are determined chiefly by ecology" and wonders if it is possible to "speak of political behavior as a distinct type of social behavior?"[61]

That last question foreshadows the foundational debates of international relations later in the century. One could trace the emergence of critical political theory and self-awareness along many paths. But Evans-Pritchard's work is possibly the first instance in which the definition of "politics" is questioned with reference to a nomadic group.

Answering his own question, Evans-Pritchard describes the consequences of the dealing with the Nuer—or anybody else—on that "more abstract plane."

> We do not, therefore, say that a man is acting politically or otherwise, but that between local groups there are relations of a structural order that can be called political.[62]

By problematizing the line between political and non-political action, Evans-Pritchard elevates what was once considered primitive. Moving cattle across pasture-land now "can be called political," rather than merely subsistence economic or developmental. It also, thus, warrants the tremendous (sometimes numbing) analysis Evans-Pritchard has conducted on everything from lineages to the bovine idiom for the preceding two hundred and fifty pages. That anthropologists spent so much time with nomadic groups in this period, and consequently took them so seriously, paved the way for an understanding of agency which we have today.

Lattimore did not immerse himself quite so deeply in a nomadic culture, but he was spiritual kin to Evans-Pritchard and the Malinowskians. In his letters he recounts with some pride his eventual mastery of the Mongol and Chinese tongues, and the modesty with which he traveled—usually in local style, with a single Mongol companion (one Arash). Even when he was traveling with his wife, on their adventurous honeymoon in 1925, he recalls that "the heaviest part of our baggage was the books we took with us."[63] That said, he did not accumulate detail like an anthropologist. He ranged widely in his geographic and temporal interests and had a concern for breadth as well as depth. In this sense, Lattimore is of greater interest from an international relations standpoint. Though his major work, *Inner Asian Frontiers of China*, was essentially a history, significant portions of it are concerned with identifying transnational patterns in the relations between nomadic and sedentary.

Lattimore argued that Chinese history was contingent upon those relations. "The need for mobility," he wrote, "produced a norm of steppe tribal society as unmistakable as the manpower norm of society in China...."[64] That norm was a continual pattern of nomadic expansion and contraction leading to a rise and fall of mixed Mongol-Chinese states on the border—what he called a "process of cracking up and sorting out." His conclusion was based largely on Chinese sources. Therein, as elsewhere, scholars were accustomed to nomads as raiders and warring tribes. Lattimore's insight was to recognize the nomadic contribution to peace. "[Their] demand for freedom...led to tribal wars, but it also made possible periods of relative stability based paradoxically on the smooth adjustment of claims to mobility."[65]

How did this work? Lattimore theorized a tension he called "wealth versus mobility." This was essentially a sliding scale between nomadism and sedentarism which governed the political stability of the Chinese frontier. One extreme, the "maximum control of mobility over wealth" was defined by large-scale nomadic invasions of China. The opposite extreme, "maximum control of wealth over mobility" described "strong dynasties in China [which] reduced nomads of the steppe to vassalage." Neither was inherently more stable. Explaining this ebb and flow, Lattimore allowed for a degree of environmental determinism, whereby eventually "farmer and herdsmen gravitated back to the geographical environment that permanently favored each of them." But he emphasized political agency—"the nomads never tired of working new combinations of mobility and wealth."

He further argued that that those two elements were inextricable from each other, and led to repeating political configurations. Here, for example, he describes the consequences of accumulation of wealth at the border, far from centralized Chinese state power, and close to the mobile population of the steppe:

> Those who were appointed to rule the frontier began to dissociate themselves from the Chinese sources of wealth...the vassal began to demand a higher price for his loyalty, resorting to his mobility to escape punishment; and thus the exploitation of wealth by mobility began again.[66]

At the opposite extreme, when the nomads conquered China, the reverse "undermining of wealth by mobility" happened like this:

> After nomadic rulers had moved to China they became detached from the sources of their power and identified with the clumsy and vulnerable apparatus of agriculture, so that when their exploitation of the settled civilization had reached the point of diminishing returns they were overwhelmed....[67]

This conception of history is remarkably similar to Ibn Khaldun's cyclical ideas about the reservoir and the city. But it is considerably more sophisticated in its analysis of nomadic behavior. When Lattimore writes that "the poor farmer could become a prosperous nomad by abandoning his underprivileged share of civilization and taking to the steppe," it is a comment on the inequity of wealth in the Chinese state and a nomadic response to it. When he continues that "'great walls,' therefore, had a function in keeping the subjects of the empires in as well as in keeping out the barbarians,"[68] he is describing the state's counter-response—its behavior towards its sedentary subjects, motivated by the attraction of nomadism.

His book thus anticipates James C. Scott's work on state projects of sedentarization and legibility—even if Lattimore's tone lacks the self-awareness that characterizes later research on the topic. He alludes to problems of definition but does not address them, for example when he touches on "the problem of when and how steppe nomadism began to operate on the inland frontier of China." "The whole problem," he writes, "could be made clearer if a distinction were habitually made between *migration* and *nomadism*. So far as I know this is not done by either Chinese or Western writers."[69]

He does not take up the task, but thinkers in the next period would grapple with such distinctions enthusiastically. By then, larger critical-theory considerations were making space in political discourse for traditionally marginalized groups like nomads. Ironically, as this space opened up, the political power of nomadism was for the first time in history diminishing significantly because of technological advances. Lattimore intuited this, and saw that the "general complex of frontier relations—the alternating increase of diminution in importance of the factor of mobility" had come within the range of "altogether new forces." "Railways entirely altered the cruder adjustments between extensive and intensive economy that had existed before."[70] Pastoral economies previously exclusive to the steppe nomad and China now opened to the Russian and Japanese states. And the railroad was not the only technology-increasing state space. Likewise firearms "alter[ed] in their own way the ratio between nomad mobility and agricultural immobility." The combined effect was that separation of Chinese sedentarists from the center of state power was reduced—mobility was less able to undermine wealth.

But this did not, in Lattimore's opinion, indicate the end of nomadism or mobility as a serious political practice. The mobile and immobile, even in this period, were "not necessarily antagonistic to each other." Indeed, he saw the new technology as an opportunity for nomadic economy. "Under modern conditions," he wrote,

> ...they can be complementary. What was lacking in the past was an adequate method of coordinating them. Industrialism and machinery can now link the steppe and the ploughman...and link them in amity and without social subordination of one people to the other.[71]

In view of the storm of *realpolitik* that engulfed Lattimore shortly after he published these words, his optimism seems almost quaint. In 1941, Chiang Kai-Shek named him his personal advisor; a year later he became deputy director of Pacific operations at the US Office of War Information. Perhaps it was his optimistic open-mindedness that landed him, in 1950, before a session of the Tydings Committee. Senator Joseph McCarthy had accused him of being the "top Soviet espionage agent in the United States." It was five years before the charges were dismissed.[72]

Had Lattimore actually been a Russian agent, he would have been in good company in our field. Soviet theorists had themselves been dealing extensively with nomads for some time. In their country the topic bred heated political discussion as early as 1934, when one Russian social scientist, S.F. Tolstov, emphasized the dangers of enacting policy regarding nomads without a coherent theoretical framework:

> This problem is by no means of merely academic significance…its solution enables us to sharpen our weapon of correct Marxist understanding…it is relevant to the immediate practice of political struggle, the practice of class war both in the Soviet East and abroad, in the colonial Orient…the correctness of the practical work of the socialist reconstruction of the nomadic and the semi-nomadic *aul* of the Soviet East depends on the correct theoretical solution of this problem….[73]

The problem he refers to is how nomadism fits into Marxism, or doesn't. Soviet scholars, drawing on their own ethnographies of the nineteenth century, were by this point constructing the first critical understandings of nomadism in relation to the state, just as Evans-Pritchard and Lattimore were. The particularities of Marxism, however, produced an extreme tension. Ernest Gellner describes it in his work on society and the state in Soviet thought.

According to Gellner, Marxist orthodoxy—with its insistence on movement towards radical social change based on class-consciousness— abhorred permanence. What then to do with nomadic society, which seemed not only unchanging and without national identity, but without class or other latent instability? The central debate was two sided. On one side, nomadic "feudalists" as Gellner puts it, did not believe land use was actually collective among nomads, but that there was monopolistic domination within nomadic society. Nomadism was thus a form of feudalism, which was an established category in the Marxist teleology. The "anti-feudalists" perceived nomads to have a genuinely communitarian, collective attitude to land use.

Gellner concluded, in 1988, that the tide of opinion in the Soviet Academy had turned to the anti-feudalists. But he was in the end less interested in the conclusion of that debate than its larger implications. His account served a larger critical study of Soviet state and ideology. Like many non-anthropological works on nomadism, his studies focused on repression to criticize a particular state.[74] He thus noted that even the anti-feudalists resolved the tensions inherent in nomadism in a radical way: "nomadic pastoralists are expelled from the dialectic of history." By way of evidence, he quotes one V.A. Shnirelman, who writes:

> In a historic perspective, the development of highly specialized societies of hunters, fisherman, and gatherers, and of nomadic pastoralists, represent dead-end branches of development.[75]

Gellner's judgement on this expulsion from history is damning. "In the 1980s, the question as to who exactly was liquidated in the steppe between the wars, and why, seems no longer to be pressing."[76] The sarcasm reflects his concern with the triumph of political expediency, ideology, and major state projects over nomads regardless of theoretical position. It finally suggests a fundamental failure of state-sponsored Soviet thought and its deadly implications for the nomadic populations of the central Asian steppe. For if the feudalists were correct, then beneath the nomadism "a feudal society was hiding, wildly signaling to be liquidated."[77] And if they were not—Gellner suggests that the anti-feudalists were themselves in danger of liquidation when the feudalists condemned them for heterodoxy.[78] The number of scholars involved in this debate—Gellner mentions major works by Vladimirtsov, Potapov, Tolstov, Tolybekov, Kabo, Markov, and half a dozen more—suggests a richness of thought that, unfortunately, has remained mostly un-translated into English.

Contemporary Comparative Anthropology

The exception was Khazanov, today a Professor Emeritus at the University of Wisconsin at Madison. He was an anti-feudalist whose ambitious work ultimately transcended the Soviet debate and became a touchstone for nomad studies. In his view, there were two sides to the field. Anthropologists had studied the nomadic communities, and historians had studied their effect on sedentary societies, usually in the form of conquest. His aim was to combine the disciplines, and his global comparative project was the first of its kind.

Khazanov's book is a broad and extraordinarily erudite survey concerned with an array of major questions. One recurring concern is inequality in nomadic versus sedentary societies and the nature of ownership. Another is the effect of nomadic invasion on the "evolution and tempo" of development, and thus the question of whether "development" is a reasonable formulation at all when comparing Chinese,

Muslim, and European societies. "[T]he frequently claimed link between the nomadic conquests and slowness of the development of the societies cited is far from simple. Slowness in comparison with what?....[I]t is doubtful every nomadic conquest inevitably slowed down the evolution of the society it conquered."[79]

Khazanov is ultimately non-committal about these large questions, and prefers to comment upon smaller arguments specific to his numerous cases. He writes in his conclusion: "all I wish to show is that there are no grounds for categoric assertions, but on the other hand there is a great deal of room for discussion and further research." However, his book does make an overarching argument:

> The book's main argument is as follows: specializations mean more dependency. The more specialized mobile pastoralists become, the more dependent they become, in turn, on the outside, non-pastoralist, mainly sedentary world....[80]

His thesis binds nomadic and sedentary societies from Ibn Khaldun's Arabia to Lattimore's China. As Khazanov puts it, "a nomadic tribe is never a purely territorial unit...foremost it is a political organization."[81] This is an explicit articulation of the idea that we have seen crudely and/or obliquely expressed throughout the subjects of this review—and it is the idea this work will apply to contemporary international relations in the following chapters.

Khazanov was not the first to make the point. Neither is he the only one to attempt a global historical comparison. There are a few other works—for example Salzman's excellent *Pastoralists* (2004), or Thomas Barfield's slim, self-described textbook *The Nomadic Alternative* (1993)—which do the same. These works draw on the anthropology of Frederick Barth, I.M. Lewis, Dawn Chatty, and William Irons, among others. All saw nomadism, sometimes at least, as explicitly political. Irons, for example, focused on nomadism as permanent political adaptation to the Persian empire in his studies of the Yomuts in the early 1970s.[82] Anthropologists like Irons delve deeply into the organization of nomadic populations and compare them not only to each other but to states. It is beyond the scope of this book to tease out the different arguments among all these anthropologists, but a key recurring question is the degree to which nomadic societies are egalitarian, democratic, or hierarchical—and what sedentary society can learn from them.

Contemporary Journalism and Philosophy

At the same time modern anthropologists were working formally on these questions, a great number of laymen began to write about nomadism. Preeminent among them was Bruce Chatwin, whose stated intentions were decidedly un-anthropological. His twenty-year effort to write a book about nomadism produced *The Songlines*. "This book is written," he wrote, "in answer to a need to explain my own restlessness."[83]

In this sense he is a direct descendant of Lawrence—the scholar "becoming" nomad. Following from Lattimore and in parallel to Scott, Chatwin also absorbed and appreciated the political agency of nomads. "The mobile rich were impossible to tax, the advantages of no fixed address were obvious."[84] He also, however, said he thought the distinction between truth and fiction "unimportant." He has endured criticism for this, but has also outgrown and outlived many social scientists working on nomadism in his period and remains a widely published novelist, travel writer, and socialite-adventurer icon. Chatwin did not have the same martial mission as Lawrence, but he did have great literary gifts and would become the most popular writer on nomads of his period. His death of unacknowledged AIDS at the age of forty-nine increased his notoriety, and sometimes distracted from his work—which is of inconsistent quality but serious intent. On nomadism his writings are very finely wrought, erudite, and incoherent. Like Herodotus and Ssu-Ma-Chi'en he traveled extensively but never dug deeply. It could be argued that Chatwin's approach is closer to the "fathers of history" than to that of his peers. He makes fantastic generalizations. Chatwin writes, for example, "the golden-brown babies of the Kalahari Bushmen hunters never cry and are among the most content babies in the world."[85] Such an assertion, in retrospect, looks downright harmful to the notion of nomadic political agency.

Chatwin, however, never said he was trying to be helpful. The stated purpose of his project was to answer a question—"why do men wander rather than sit still?" His answer, *The Songlines*, is a kaleidoscopic account of some time spent with Australian Aboriginals and includes a large and disparate collection of fragments—primary, secondary, and of his own device—which reflect decades of inchoate work on the topic. His essay "It's a Nomad, *Nomad*, World," for example, opens with a quote from Pascal, and the following argument: "Diversion. Distraction. Fantasy. Change of fashion, food, love and landscape. We need them as the air we breathe. Without change our brains and bodies rot. The man who sits quietly in a shatered [sic] room is likely to be mad, tortured by hallucinations and introspection." After Pascal, he mentions Montaigne, Li-Po, Proust, Louis-Stevenson, Robert Burt, Mohammed, John the Baptist, Whitman, Rumi—never for more than a line or two. He notes that dervishes—presumably nomadic—believed they were flying. He asserts "all of our activities are linked to the ideas of journeys." He compares nomadism to dancing and then reminds us that "during the French Revolution Paris went on one of the great dancing sprees in history."

His observations on nomad-state relations are rarer than these literary digressions, which are romantic, dramatic, but an awful lot of fun. They illustrate how fully the myth of the nomad had been turned on its head in Chatwin's world. Rather than feared, nomads were lauded by children of the dominant aristocracy, an object of gap year fascination even among the auction houses and newspapers that Chatwin worked for. None of this precluded critical thinking, exactly. "The word nomad must go," Chatwin writes in one letter. "It is too vague unless used in the strictest sense, that is a 'wandering herdsman,' and too loaded with emotional prejudices...."[86] But in the end critical political thinking wasn't really the point. Chatwin's problems were explicitly existential[87]—one of his collections is titled, "What am I doing here?" As his biographer Nicholas Shakespeare writes: "say almost anything of Bruce Chatwin and the opposite is also true."

This ambiguity separated him from most anthropologists, but united him with two major[88] philosophers working on nomadism. French philosophers Gilles Deleuze and Félix Guattari aggressively co-opt the idea of nomadism and inflate its importance to an almost absurd degree. Their work seems at times willfully obscure. As Brian Massumi asks in his introduction to *A Thousand Plateaus*, "what do you do with a book that dedicates an entire chapter to music and animal behavior—and then claims that it isn't a chapter?"[89] That kind of contradiction is everywhere in "1227: Treatise on Nomadology." The chapter discusses states and nomads through a series of "axioms," "propositions," and "problems," without ever defining its aim, or even several of its terms. For example: "Axiom I. The war machine is exterior to the State apparatus. Proposition I. This exteriority is first attested to in mythology, epic, drama, and games."[90] While the "war machine" is much discussed through the chapter, it is never defined. This is of a piece with the rest of the book's radical arguments: "to attribute the book to a subject is to overlook this working of matters, and the exteriority of their relations. It is to fabricate a beneficient God to explain geological movements."[91] The language is so abstruse that it is difficult to draw any conclusions from it, though it frequently references nomadism and the state directly:

> *Problem I.* Is there a way of warding off the formation of a State apparatus (or its equivalents in a group)? *Proposition II.* The exteriority of the war machine is also attested to by ethnology (a tribute to the memory of Pierre Clastres).[92]

Clastres was one of the pioneers of nomadism as political practice. But their use of him here is lost in convoluted prose and begs the question: what are Deleuze and Guattari doing with "nomadism," and is there any value in it?

Massumi suggests that they use the word to string together an apparently disparate philosophical tradition:

> [Deleuze] discovered an orphan line of thinkers who were tied by no direct descendance but were united in their opposition to the State philosophy... Between Lucretius, Hume, Spinoza, Nietzsche, and Bergos there exists a 'secret link constituted by the critique of negativity, the cultivation of joy, the hatred of interiority, the exteriority of forces and relations, the denunciation of power....' [Deleuze] crossfertilized that line of 'nomad' thought with contemporary theory."[93]

There is much that is unclear even in Massumi's explanation. But it suggests what Deleuze might have meant by the term "nomad." It seems to have little to do with nomads and their lives today—and more to do with the history of philosophy. But the idea of nomadism can be as powerful as any great wall. It is fair to say that the philosophers' work reflects a vanguard[94] notion of nomadism as political expression. And it is this idea that the book will now pursue in the international relations subfields of security, trade, and climate change.

3

BYWAYS NOT CONTROLLED

THE SECURITIZATION OF PERPETUAL MOBILITY

"How is the armed struggle this morning?"
"The struggle continues."

Common Greeting,
Tigrayan People's Liberation Front

This chapter explores some of the relationships between nomadism and global security. It begins by briefly examining the representation of nomadism in Western media before defining securitization and providing an example of a state-nomadic relationship that was not highly securitized. It then illustrates how, why, and with what consequences states and international actors so frequently securitize nomadic populations, and how those populations respond. The sedentary actors in this relation commonly conceive of nomadism in some combination of the following five forms: i) as an existential threat to sovereignty; ii) as an asset in military campaigns; iii) as a strategy of reconciliation; iv) as an incubator of terrorism and criminality; or v) as an inseparable element of racial identity. The chapter examines each form—mostly in Sudan, Afghanistan, and the Western Saharan States, but drawing on instances from around the world—before concluding with an argument for nomadism's place in "new wars" theory.

THE CIVILIZATION OF PERPETUAL MOVEMENT

Mobility as an Existential Threat

In 2006, *The Boston Globe* published an article titled "UN Council Feels Heat for Peace in Darfur" that contained the following paragraph:

> ...clashes in Darfur over land and water erupted into war in early 2003 when ethnic African rebels based in farming villages rose up against Sudan's Arab-led government, which responded by unleashing nomadic Arab militias known as janjaweed.[1]

This is common language in media coverage of the Darfur conflict. The image particularly of "unleashing" the nomads appears repeatedly, across the political spectrum: Reuters,[2] Fox News,[3] *The Scotsman*,[4] *The New York Times*,[5] *USA Today*,[6] the Associated Press[7] and others have all employed it. While writers for major Western media outlets frequently problematize broad categories like Arab and African, the categories of nomad and farmer are not so regularly complicated—especially when they arise in the context of war. The implication of "unleashing" is that nomads are inherently aggressive, as little capable of political decision-making as a dog on a chain. It denies them agency. Even when experienced reporters and analysts interview nomadic populations, they often produce material that caters to conventional, indeed romantic, notions of nomadism. *The New York Times*, for example, provided valuable coverage of the conflict in Darfur. And yet in 2005, it published an article with the de-politicizing title "Leading Player in Darfur's Drama: The Hapless Camel"—even as the reporter explicitly referenced the complexities facing nomads.[8]

Nomadism can safely remain an object of fascination for the media. But for states and international organizations, it has direct, quantifiable, and often violent consequences. The "Mongol Horde's" flow in and out of the Chinese state is archetypical. In more recent centuries, equally vivid examples are less well known. In most cases, nomads and state or interstate actors do more than conquer one another—they exploit each other, co-opt each other, and sometimes move along the spectrum from sedentary to nomadic simultaneously.

The Orang Laut of Southeast Asia are an excellent example. The anthropologist Clifford Sather writes that in the colonial period their "boat Nomadism [wa]s embedded in a complex political order....Various named groups of Orang Laut were incorporated in the Kingdom of Johore by their formalized ties to the ruler. These ties were articulated in terms of the specific corvée duties assigned to each group (*'suku'*). With corvée duties (*'kerahan'*) were associated degrees of status."[9] Fighting was one of these duties—but not necessarily the most important. According to Leonard Andaya, a historian of Southeast Asia:

> ...The duties of the Orang Laut were to gather sea products for the China trade, perform certain special services for the ruler at weddings, funerals, or on a hunt, serve as transport for envoys and royal missives, man the ships and serve as a fighting force on the ruler's fleet, and patrol the waters of the Kingdom. Except in times of actual warfare when their services were needed for the fleet, the Orang Laut were usually on patrol providing protection for Johor's traders or to those wanting to trade in Johor while harassing all other shipping....[10]

In various ways, then, the Orang Laut were allied with a state—without being yoked to it in the same way as the sedentary, cultivating populations of Johore and neighboring pre-colonized kingdoms.[11] With the decline of the Johore state in the eighteenth century, the Orang Laut continued to flourish as an independent, though never monolithic, group—"appear[ing] to have transferred their allegiance to local Malay chieftains..."[12]

The expansion of the British North Borneo Company (BNBC) changed the situation. For the BNBC, the Orang Laut were not one of several articulated *sukus* with specialized *kerehan*. Instead they were a threat, existential and clear. They were pirates. As one of the BNBC's district officers, J.H. Molyneux, wrote in the *British North Borneo Herald* in 1902:

> In conclusion I would suggest that all Bajaus be...removed to one settlement approachable by boat, from which there are less means of escape than from an island surrounded by extensive coral reefs....There is no reason why Bajaus should not cease their roving, piratical habits and become a steady settled people.[13]

For Molyneux, roving habits are inherently piratical, and the benefits of settlement obvious. His superior, Governor Birch, was less restrained: "They are the terror of everyone—Piracy, robbing on the high seas and on land and murder are of common occurrence and the lawless people own no authority and pay no taxes."[14] The company's sedentarization schemes—from boat-registration to the encouragement of coconut cultivation—all restricted mobility on this basis. Following from this, "one of the consequences of repression of piracy in the mid-nineteenth century was a rapid sedentarization of a number of these groups."[15] These restrictions resemble processes Scott describes across Southeast Asia. Sather's description of boat registration, for instance, in which:

> ...The Company introduced in 1901 a system of boat licensing.... For the next decade virtually all the government's involvement in the district was occupied with enforcing boat registration. The system had three main purposes. The first...was to register native vessels.... The second was revenue collection. In licensing his vessel, each boat-owner was required to pay a licensing fee amounting in most cases to one dollar per annum. The fee was treated as a substitute for a head or house tax imposed elsewhere...on more settled people. Finally, payment of this fee was looked upon as an acknowledgment of company sovereignty...[16]

These are what Scott would call processes of legibility. In order to exert control over a population, a state/MNC first tries to count it, classify it—that is, make it legible. The problem for a nomadic population is that to count it, the state/MNC needs to sedentarize it—and to do that, securitize it. The Orang Laut, of course, were not all pirates.

It is conceivable that the BNBC could have incorporated the mobility of the Orang Laut into their political conception in a variety of ways, just as the Sultanate of Johore and the Malay Chiefs did. Instead, they simply "presented [them] as an existential threat, requiring emergency measures and justifying actions outside the normal bounds of political procedure."[17] That is—to use Buzan's definition—they securitized[18] them. This process—in which the sedentary securitize the nomadic, and that securitization leads to sedentarization—is a pattern of behavior between sedentary states and nomadic peoples from which the Sultanate was an exception.

Why does this pattern exist? Today it occurs most commonly for instrumental reasons, as we shall see. But prior to that, conceptually and historically, the "security studies" explanation is that states actually do perceive nomadism as an existential threat. As Buzan, Waever, and Wilde put it:

> ...existential threats are traditionally defined in terms of the constituting principle—sovereignty, but sometimes also ideology—of the state. Sovereignty can be threatened by anything that questions recognition, legitimacy, or governing authority....International regimes, and international society more broadly, can be existentially threatened by situations that undermine the rules, norms, and institutions that constitute those regimes.[19]

Nomadism is perceived as such a threat because some fundamental powers of the state system—taxes, conscription, border regulation, for example—depend upon stationary populations.[20] As Molyneux writes of his settlement scheme: "If [it] was done, they could be made to pay their boat taxes, could be induced to take out passes for hunting jungle produce like other natives, and would be forced to desist in slave dealing...."[21] Deviation from these practices threatens the BNBC—which responds, unsurprisingly, by attempting to diminish the threat. Sedentarization was, and remains, the ultimate elimination of the threat of nomadism.

These nomad-specific processes also fit within a larger narrative of colonial encounter. However, while many of the concepts underlying that encounter have since been discarded or at least problematized in the security discourse, nomadism remains frequently, un-reflectively securitized.

Reports by the political officers of United States Foreign Service reflect the processes' continued dominance. Their securitization of the Kuchis—a population of two to three million predominantly Pashtun nomads who range across the Pakistan-Afghanistan border—is not radically different from Molyneux's of the Orang Laut. The Kuchis came to the attention of the US military following its 2003 invasion of Afghanistan. Representative cables do not outright securitize them on the basis of shared ethnicity with the majority of the Taliban—the US's enemy—but they do categorize mobility as a "security dimension" above and beyond the "conflict":

> There is a security dimension to the conflict as the Kuchi can be vulnerable to recruitment by the Taliban: they travel from Waziristan into Ghazni, Wardak and elsewhere along byways that are not controlled by recognized security forces.[22]

There is accuracy in the broader assessment, which emerges later in the cable: poorer, less well-educated Afghans—like the Kuchis—are indeed more likely to be recruited into the insurgency. In that analysis, the US Foreign Service has moved beyond Molyneux. But for the BNBC and the US both, the Orang Laut and the Kuchis are defined by their mobility—whether "roving, piratical," "own[ing] no authority,"[23] or "travel[ing] byways not controlled by recognized security forces." They present an existential problem. Like Molyneux's report, a US cable ultimately suggests solving it like this:

> The...permanent solution of this problem lies in implementation of Article 14 of the Constitution of Afghanistan, which obliges the government of

Afghanistan to…execute effective programs for the development of agriculture and livestock, improvement of economic conditions and livelihood of farmers and cattle raisers *and for the resettlement of Kuchies*.[24]

This argument for settlement as an antidote to violence is often couched in the "apolitical" terms of improving Kuchi access to services and education:

…to permanently solve this problem and prevent violent clashes among Afghan tribes in the future, particularly between Kuchi and locals, the government *should start new projects of distributing barren government lands and settling landless farmers and Kuchi there*, so they can get out of the miserable life and…their children can have access to education.

"Barren" here mistakenly posits a *terra nullius*, but "the miserable life," is not a neo-colonial invention. It is often cold, unsanitary, hungry, and dangerous to be a Kuchi. Best estimates place literacy rates for men at 14 per cent; for women, 3 per cent.[25] But the securitization of populations based on mobility throws up numerous problems. It rejects, ignores, limits, or overlooks the active political nature of nomadism. It can be noted here also that it is not only colonial powers and Western states which securitize and attempt to sedentarize nomads. Non-Western states have a similarly long history of doing this, as do non-Western, non-state actors—even some of the most "radical." To take one example—in Ethiopia in the 1970s, the Tigrayan People's Liberation Front (TPLF) attempted to sedentarize a population of Afars in order to satisfy its recruitment needs and resource requirements.[26] The pattern of securitization into sedentarization knows no geography, no ideology.

The Material Military Value of Nomadism

That pattern does, however have its basis in real threats posed by nomadism. As Buzan and Waever point out, securitization is inter-subjective—it is easier to securitize a heavily armed, bellicose neighbor than a lightly armed, peaceful one. Nomads are especially susceptible to securitization because their mode of life is foreign to the sedentary majority. But it is also true that some of the practices which render nomads susceptible to securitization do indeed make them agile and powerful in armed conflict, especially in areas of limited state control.

"The Mongol Horde" again provides the archetypical example, but nomadic military capacity is apparent throughout the twentieth century and still today. As Peter Little notes early in his book *Somalia: Economy Without State*,

> In the past 20 years alone numerous political resistance movements in Africa (e.g. Algeria, Ethiopia, Kenya, Mali, Somalia, Sudan, and Uganda) and elsewhere (e.g. Afghanistan, China, Iraq, Israel, Pakistan, Turkey, and Yemen) have emerged in pastoral[27] areas that have been economically and politically discriminated against, as well as forcefully subjugated to foreign political structures and at times compulsory settlement.[28]

In each of those movements, a militarized wing informed by nomadism—if not outright comprised of nomads—has emerged. The value of nomads in a military context is obvious. Mobility, local knowledge, and cost efficiency manifest themselves in resistance movements of the kind Little mentions. Among the most spectacular examples is the Bedouin capture of Aqaba[29] in the Arab Revolt of 1916–18, in which camel mounted irregulars traveled overland to take the critical seaport. To name only a handful of groups that have engaged in similar action more recently: The Afar Revolutionary Democratic Unity Front on the Ethiopian-Eritrean Border (ARDUF), the Taliban in Afghanistan and Pakistan, the MNLA and other Tuareg groups in West Africa, the Sudanese Revolutionary Front (SRF) and other Janjaweed groups across the Sahel—all have taken advantage of nomadism in their respective conflicts.

Interested actors capitalize on the attendant sedentary fears. The Director General (DG) of the Independent Directorate of Kuchis (IDK) in Kabul, Abdul Wahab Sulemankheil, for example, estimated to an American political officer that

> ...over 1/2 of Taliban are Kuchis....For example, in his home province of Paktika, the majority of Taliban commanders are Kuchis. (Comment: The Other Government Agency[30] office estimates Kuchis comprise only a single-digit percentage of the Taliban. The DG may be inflating the participation of the Kuchis in the Taliban movement to ensure Kuchi interests are considered in any peace-promotion efforts. End Comment).[31]

Conversely, and perhaps more surprisingly for the mainstream conception, instrumentalization of nomadism is just as common in counter-insurgency. Indeed nomads are among the most effective counter-insurgents. Alex de Waal refers to the alliance between the Government of Sudan and certain nomadic groups in Darfur as "counter-insurgency on the cheap."[32] The Ethiopian government was able to make peace with the ARDUF long enough to benefit from their tactics during the Ethiopian-

Eritrean war of 1998–2000.[33] And when the Taliban controlled the Afghan state apparatus themselves, nomadism was useful in their own efforts. Sulemankheil raises a similar possibility for the Americans:

> Citing the success of Kuchi tribal forces against the Taliban in Pakistan's Swat Valley, the DG suggested that tribal security forces…should be empowered to defend local communities and reconcile against the Taliban in Afghanistan.[34]

This is not a notion original to Sulemankheil. The United States has dedicated enormous resources to similar ideas as part of the overhaul of its counter-insurgency doctrine.[35] As David Kilcullen, the principal author of the United States Counter-Insurgency Handbook, plainly notes:

> …our pursuit of terrorists that has brought us into sustained contact with traditional nonstate social hierarchies—Wazirs, Mashuds, Kuchi, Albu Mahal, Janabi, Tuareg—whose geographic and demographic terrain interest Western governments mainly because terrorists hide (or a are believed to hide) in it.[36]

Many of these non-state groups are nomadic. For the last decade, the US and international community have been especially pre-occupied with the relevant "terrain" in Afghanistan and Pakistan. And in dealing with the relevant nomads, the Kuchis, they have not only presented nomadism as an existential threat to local authority, they have recognized its significant military capacity.

Nomads As Reconciliating Agents in "Humanitarian Intervention"

More surprisingly, the international community sometimes attempts to take advantage of nomadic agility in reconciliation attempts during "humanitarian intervention." In the run up to these events, however, actively constructed identities determine nomadic contribution to a conflict and reconciliation. Taking the Afghan case again, Kuchis are located in the traditionally oversimplified narrative of nomad versus farmer. As a spokesman for the Afghanistan Independent Human Rights Commission puts it: "this problem recurs every year."[37] The idea that the conflict has immemorial roots in resource competition is frequently echoed in the press reports and political actor analysis. American Embassy cables, for example, also state that the conflict is "annual."[38]

While it is true that in recent summers violence has recurred in the Hazarajat, it would be more accurate to say that the threat of conflict has been annual. There have also been periods of peace. Conflict is neither inevitable nor contingent simply upon quantity and availability of water and pasture. These factors contribute, but they do not determine. Moreover, the relevant actors capitalize upon the excessive explanatory power of the simple myth. Hazara leaders insist that "[they] have been repressed by the more numerous Pashtuns for centuries—a situation which the Kuchis are trying to perpetuate."[39] A majority of Hazaras are sedentary, but from their base in the Hazarajat a diaspora has emerged which fights for the ear of the Anglophone international community with communication resources that the Kuchis cannot muster. The Hazara community has websites, for example, which trade on stereotypical notions of the barbaric nomad.[40] In this context, as IRIN News reports:

> Kuchi elders complain that since the overthrow of the Taliban government in 2001, Hazaras have enjoyed strong international support and been given opportunities in the government and other decision-making bodies, while Kuchis have been perceived as collaborators of the mainly Pashtun Taliban and "terrorists."[41]

Officials of the US led intervention, of course, claim to treat the various "ethnic" groups equally.[42]

They fail to do so at their peril. History has often shown that securitization of a population based on ethnic identity is incoherent, normatively flawed, and ultimately dangerous.[43] Especially in terms of reconciliation, it is at least as constructive to consider the current situation in terms of nomadism as ethnicity. As one US Embassy cable put it:

> Defining "a Kuchi voter" for future elections is a thorny political question. Ethnic Pashtuns now hold all 10 Kuchi seats. Ethnic Turkmen, Tajiks, and Baluchi also are possible Kuchi voters, however, because Afghans accept that "Kuchi" refers to the nomadic way of life rather than a distinct ethnic group. Yet the Kuchis' increasingly settled existence and the competition for resources this creates…lies behind some of the present friction between Kuchis and other groups.[44]

It is a lesson in *real-politik* that so many Afghans exploit ethnic politics—as above in the Hazara-Kuchi discourse—even if, as rightly reported above, they prioritize nomadism over ethnicity. Prioritized or not, local, national, and international actors all recognize the immediate relevance of nomadism for resolving the war and state-building enterprise of the previous decade. And they are all trying to take advantage of the situation.

The process can be read in a June 2009 US Embassy cable titled "Local Kuchi-Hazara Deal Dependent On National And International

Actors" which specified local negotiations towards a cessation of violence. It reported the emergence of an agreement

> ...under which the Kuchi will not migrate to their traditional pastures in Wardak's Behsud district, but rather remain in empty lands further east in Daymirdad district, and will publicly support the elections process. In return, the governor and the locals agreed among themselves that the international community should provide humanitarian assistance to the Kuchi, while the Independent Election Commission (IEC) should provide assurances for Kuchi voting....[45]

Though this cable initially reported the conflict to be annual, here it reports on flexibility and political dependency—contradicting the nomad-farmer inevitability narrative. Moreover, it reports that Kuchi mobility decisions are contingent upon processes—election logistics and international aid—dominated by the US and its partners in the International Security Assistance Force (ISAF). The report conclude that if the highlighted agreement held, it would "yield security benefits,"—ISAF's primary objective. And that agreement explicitly requires engagement with the nomadic population in terms of modified mobility outside of an "annual" conflict. Thus, even as actors securitize nomadism as a static root of conflict—in the apolitical farmer/herder binary—Kuchi behavior forces them to deal with nomadism as political expression.

Nomads as Terrorists

Nomadism is most frequently associated with a particular threat: terrorism. In the Sahara, as in Afghanistan, the dominant narrative in the Anglophone security discourse is that the region, as George W. Bush put it, "has become a frontline in the war on terror."[46] Weak states and vast, uncontrollable spaces provide safe haven for violent, radicalized Islamist elements from around the world. The narrative is not limited to the hawkish American Right. Democratic Senator Russ Feingold and others on the Left have emphasized it as well:

> The [Obama] administration is right to focus attention on the Pakistan-Afghanistan region, but we cannot lose sight of other places where al-Qaeda is seeking to gain ground. As we have seen in Somalia and Yemen, weak states, chronic instability, ungoverned spaces and unresolved local tensions can create almost ideal safe havens in which terrorists can recruit and operate. Several parts of the Sahel region include that same mix of ingredients. And

the danger they pose, not just to regional security, but to our own national security, is real.[47]

This opinion is not limited to the United States. Al Jazeera reports that "Richard Barrett of the UN's al-Qaeda–Taliban monitoring team said that while attacks by al-Qaeda and its operatives were decreasing in many parts of the world, the situation was worsening in North Africa," and especially the Sahel.[48] Much of the mainstream news media has buttressed this idea: a 2009 *New York Times* feature, "The Saharan Conundrum," for example, featured the subhead, "Much of Mauritania is empty—a laboratory for terrorists and their hunters."[49]

The Sahel is not, of course, "empty." Nomads populate the imagined *terra nullius*. A counter narrative has been developing which questions the significance of any armed Islamist movements related to al-Qaeda in the area (AQIM);[50] suggests that they are exaggerated; or even attributes their very existence to the US led securitization of the region.[51] One of the most radical—and widely respected[52]—proponents of this counter narrative, Jeremy Keenan, suggests that in 2003 the US actually staged a kidnapping to create an AQIM bogey-man, for the following reason:

> AQIM, far from being a threat to the West, is more of an adjunct to the West's overall strategies in the region. It provides the US with further justification for AFRICOM while providing European powers, notably France whose nuclear industry is powered by the Sahel's uranium, with the justification to intervene militarily in the resource-rich corridor of the Sahel.[53]

In these competing narratives, and across the range of perspectives between them,[54] nomadism plays a crucial role—even when overlooked. Actors and theorists who address the Saharan population directly often instrumentalize perceptions of nomads at the expense of nomadic agency. Moreover—in so far as it is possible to dissociate perceptions from "on the ground" reality—these actors are engaged with the Saharan nomadic population in military and diplomatic operations, with consequences for issues ranging from the energy economy of West Africa to the lives of hostages. Nomadism partly dictates the regional security situation. But the relations between ideational and material factors and the complexity of nomadic agency[55] are lost in the grander narratives.

They are clearer in specific incidents. In late January 2004, for example, two Swiss, one German, and one British tourist were ambushed and taken captive by Tuaregs on the Niger-Mali border. The tourists were returning from a "festival of nomad culture."[56] The Tuaregs who captured them can be said to fit clearly into the dominant narrative account in which

> ...analysis of GSPC/AQIM's Saharan expansion notes the Group's involvement in smuggling of arms, cigarettes, and other contraband, as well as human trafficking, all practices that are widespread in the un-policed desert region. Routes carrying people, weapons, drugs, and especially tobacco cross the Sahara to Europe, typically directed by Tuareg nomads using SUVs and cell phones.[57]

But these Tuaregs also fit into an interpretation less focused on the direct agency of AQIM/S: "that the Tuaregs' interaction with AQIM is likely based more on economic interests, not ideological similarities."[58] American cables concerning the incident adopt a view somewhere between the two interpretations: "The crisis teams now in Bamako face a short window of opportunity to try to negotiate the release of the captives before they are turned over to a "buyer"—likely AQIM.[59]

The turn over to the "buyer" clearly dissociates the kidnappers from the AQIM. But a potentially transactional relationship provided reason enough to securitize the population. In 2009, for example, the US donated to Mali "modern military vehicles and communications equipment for improved intelligence and surveillance, especially of northern Mali, home to nomadic Tuareg."[60] The cable also recommended engagement outside official channels, thereby undermining developing state legitimacy:

> We believe they must immediately engage local Tuareg leaders from the Gao and Menaka areas to solicit advice and request assistance; the Europeans must broaden their contacts beyond President Toure, Sissoko and Coulibaly to certain individuals at other levels of the Malian government who have both the ability to influence events on the ground in Gao and Menaka....[61]

The result of such a combination of actions, critics argue, is an increase in "North African-Sahelian governments...branding indigenous Saharan groups as having links to 'armed Islamic groups', 'dissidents' and 'terrorists'." As Konstantina Isidoros asks: "When US officials court these governments, who will not jump onboard the development handout wagon?"[62]

In this context, it is ironic that the process of information collection which dictates those handouts/decisions itself depends upon members of the securitized population. In regard to the January 2009 kidnapping:

Ousmane's[63] name was the first given to the Embassy by another Taghat Melet Tuareg on January 24 after nomads reported seeing 4 westerners covered with hoods in the back of a truck north east of Anderamboukane....

The embassy in Bamako communicated via these Taghat Melet intermediaries throughout the incident. Reports to the Embassy from one of them, Sikabar Ag Ouefene, illustrate the direct relationship between perceptual securitization of a nomadic population and a trans-national hostage negotiation. In one dispatch,

> ...Ag Ouefene said he and ag Meyda attempted to reassure Mohamed and encourage him to *work toward releasing the hostages for his own sake and that of fellow Tuaregs who fear that Mali or westerners will use this crisis to portray all Tuaregs as sympathizers of Al Qaeda in the Lands of the Islamic Mahgreb (AQIM)*. Ag Ouefene reportedly told Mohamed to try to find a solution that did not involve passing the tourists to AQIM and to focus not on an eventual pay-off but on his own future.[64]

Ouefene's argument is predicated on an attempt to un-securitize an identity. But he makes it on behalf of the actors who securitized that identity in the first place.

Were the kidnappers intimately affiliated with AQIM, as the dominant narrative would have it? Or were they instead, as some critics suggest, "desert nomads with no option but to fight...to recuperate their indigenous land—land that they are denied access to by corrupt governments in receipt of US development aid; land upon which US-contracted uranium extraction now occurs"?[65] Either way, they were political agents in a Saharan system alien to a hegemon which, impoverished in its conceptions of the region and nomadism, securitized them. Understanding this, members of their community not only used injustices in the discourse to manipulate a hostage situation, but presented the correction of that discourse as an outcome comparable in value to cash and the lives of hostages.

In the moment, none of this was clear. AQIM exploited the moment by taking credit for the crime. And just as critics of the dominant discourse overlook key systems like nomadism when they make generalizations that

> ...any political resurgence[66] that uses symbols of Islam is reported as manifestations of 'Islamic fundamentalism/extremism/terrorism'...

...so too did AQIM generalize, when it released this statement:

> The British captive was killed so that he, and with him the British state, may taste a tiny portion of what innocent Muslims taste every day at the hands of the crusader and Jewish coalition to the east and to the west....[67]

The victim, Edwin Dyer, 60, of Reading, would probably have been more inclined to accept the first set of generalizations, but it is no longer possible for him to say.

Some nomads who are the objects of these securitizing generalizations are also vocal opponents of them—especially among the Tuareg community. Not all Tuaregs are nomads, but in the process of securitization the distinction has become blurred—just as it is blurred for some Tuaregs themselves. Assan Midal, for example, directs an NGO dedicated to education in Nimaey, Niger, and works as a guide in the Sahara. "Certain people say," he told *France 24*,

> ...that there is complicity between the Tuaregs and AQIM. We cannot say that the opposite is true, nor claim that this does not concern us. But be careful not to treat the Tuaregs and AQIM as if they were one. More than being a political problem, this problem is linked to contempt for our culture.[68]

The breakdown of distinct identities he bemoans is a function of securitization and a problem for nomads as a category. In this sense he is correct about it being a cultural problem: as we have seen, the mobility of his culture, nomadism itself—makes him a likely target of securitization. Ultimately, however, his awareness of this problem does not inoculate him against making the same kind of mistake. One of his appeals, for example, runs like this:

> In our opinion, the CEO of Areva [Anne Lauvergeon] represents France. And France doesn't trust us. The French have lived with us for 40 years and we deserve their respect. A Tuareg has never kidnapped a French citizen. We cannot fight against France. All we can do is demand that our rights are respected, and that the great powers stop ignoring our way of life.

He presents an opinion which plays off perceptions of the strict connections between states and MNCs (and colonialism) as much as the states play off myths of apolitical nomadism. Areva does not "represent France" any more than the Sahara is "empty" or nomads are "ungovernable." Rather, Lauvergeon (at that time) was the CEO of an MNC with majority French state investment. She thus represented multiple investors—Siemens, for example—not simply the French state. Midal's cloudy perceptions of MNCs and states equals theirs of him. State misperception of Midal, however, leads to a presumption of terrorism.

Nomads, Racial Conflict, and UN Resolution 1556

These confused perceptions are occasionally codified at the highest levels of international security policy. United Nations Resolution 1556, for example, represents a misunderstanding of nomadism in the Darfur region. In it, the Security Council

> ...*Demands* that the Government of Sudan fulfill its commitments to disarm the Janjaweed militias and apprehend and bring to justice Janjaweed leaders and their associates who have incited and carried out human rights and international humanitarian law violations and other atrocities....[69]

The problems with the "resolution to disarm the Janjaweed," as it was widely known, stemmed from blurry conceptions of who the nomadic Janjaweed were, and why they were fighting. The UN report on statements of Security Council members following the resolution stated that the Sudanese government was "exploiting an ancient rivalry between Arab African herdsmen and groups of largely black African farmers."[70] This oversimplifies nomadism and binds it to a simplistic racial analysis. As Mahmoud Mamdani argues[71]

> ...The janjawid are a nomadic phenomenon, not an 'Arab' one. Born of destitution and political strife, this phenomenon runs through the entire span of the Sahel, from Darfur to Chad and the Central African Republic and beyond....[It] emerged from the crisis of nomadism against the backdrop of a colonial power hostile to nomadism...."[72]

Mamdani is one of several historians who have worked to tell the story of the Janjaweed. He emphasizes their poverty and lawlessness; Alex de Waal emphasizes their tension with successive states:

> From the time of the sultans, the camel herding Abbala Rizeigat had been a headache to the rulers of Darfur. They refused to stay in the places allotted to them, and had no paramount chief to keep them in order....[T]he status of the Abbala Rizeigat in Darfur's tribal hierarchy was never resolved, fuelling a cycle of tribal conflicts and economic grievances that culminated in the emergence of the janjawiid....[73]

For both historians, the ancient Arab nomad vs. African famer idea is problematic. And yet, in 2004, that over-simplified conception can be read in the Security Council resolution. This conception quickly compounds the problems of racial politics by limiting the agency of and potential political dialogue between the "herders" and "farmers." As

Mamdani writes, "the history of the cattle and the camel nomads needs to be understood on its own terms and not as part of a general history of 'the Arabs of Sudan,' one that risks lumping together the history of settled and nomadic peoples, those in power and those marginal to it, in a single indistinguishable flow."[74]

This was never more apparent than in 2007, when one of the leading Arab Janjaweed chiefs, Hamdan Hemeti, broke with the Government of Sudan and signed a memorandum of understanding (MOU) with Abdelwahid Al-Nur's Darfur rebel group, the Sudanese Liberation Movement (SLM)—some of the very people he had been accused of committing racially motivated genocide against. After the switch, Hemeti was among the most serious threats facing the Sudanese government's campaign in Darfur. Thus, disarming nomadic Janjaweed like Hemeti, even had it been possible, would have further endangered the civilian population of Darfur that the resolution was trying to protect. Disarming Hemeti at the height of his alleged crimes, or prior to them, would of course have been ideal. However, the resolution—ubiquitously recognized as un-enforceable in the short term—left no room for negotiation with men like Hemeti following his conversion. It was too informed by mistaken ideas about how political a Janjaweed—a nomad—could be in the context of a "racial" conflict.

It could be argued that, no matter, the international pressure contributed to Hemeti's conversion. But explanations for such groups' behavior are numerous and varied. According to the intelligence report on Hemeti's motivations based on a clandestine meeting in 2008,[75] he cited "the long grievances of the Aballa Rezeigat that their community lacks far behind in development and the provision of basic social services such as water, health, education, etc." Conversely, the report noted that:

> Even though Hamdan appeared to have been genuine at the time, many Darfurians whom CA spoke to indicated that the motive behind the rebellion of Arab militia against the government was not based on genuine political grievances, historical injustices and marginalization, but was solely motivated by greed to extract more financial and political concessions from the government.[76]

Both explanations support Mamdani's assertion that "as a social phenomenon, the Janjaweed are an expression of the crisis of nomadism across the entire Sahelian belt" as much as any concept of racial superiority. Whatever the explanation, there is no better evidence against the oversimplified "Arab nomad vs. African farmer" concept then Hemeti's conversion from *genocidaire* into rebel. That he switched again, later in the year, only emphasizes nomadic agency.

In spite of all this, according to Mamdani, "those who blew the whistle on Darfur in 2004 have continued to argue that the violence in Darfur is racially motivated, perpetrated by 'light skinned Arabs' on 'black Africans'...[and] this kind of framing of violence continues the error that came out the colonial tradition of racializing the peoples of Sudan."[77] The same is true of the nomad vs. farmer framing. As with the association of Taliban and Kuchis on the basis of Pashtun identity, the securitization of the Janjaweed of Darfur in the last decade tended to associate nomads exclusively with Arab identity—even though Fur, Maasalit, and Zaghawa peoples are all known to live as nomads. The UN Office for the Coordination of Humanitarian Affairs, for example, described the Janjaweed as "horse and camel-riding Arab nomads, opportunists and 'criminals.'"[78] Other examples are numerous in the press and international NGO community.[79]

The confusion cannot, however, be attributed solely to a securitizing international establishment. As in the Kuchi case, the local actors take advantage of a loaded ethnic discourse for potential gain. As Alex de Waal put it regarding some of the Arab militias in Darfur in 2008:

> Interesting how at one point these people can say with total conviction that they want to eradicate Darfur's African tribes and the next moment say that the government is treacherous and they will fight it to the last...[80]

UN reports[81] and a few pieces of journalism[82] corroborate this in terms of the movement of military resources and loyalties. That said, the relationship between nomadism and ethnic identity is not straightforwardly instrumental in the process of securitization. Some of the violence was clearly framed in simplistic racial terms, but Mamdani must be qualified. The complexity of the situation can be teased out by considering statements of the alleged Janjaweed war criminal Musa Hilal in the context of de Waal's analysis.

While the UN and press mostly imply that the fighting nomads are all Arab, and motivated by racial solidarity, de Waal, critically, argues that the conflict is a result of marginalization and complex relations between center and periphery. And Hilal, when asked in interview "who will represent the interests of the Arabs at the peace talks?" says this:

To solve this problem by talking Arab wishes and others wishes, I do not agree with this, it will not solve the problem. All the movements should sit, but to divide the conference between Arab and non-Arab now, this is the first division. And you will not bring them back.

His rejection of ethnic politics can be read as support for de Waal's interpretation. Hilal claims to be wary of reductionist identity politics and its damaging effects. But later in the same interview, Hilal says the following, referring to his Fur nemesis Abdelwahid al-Nur:

All the accidents that have happened are against Arabs. When he says he is not against Arabs it is not true because he has done many accidents against Arabs....But he has developed and now he has stormed his mind as he has gotten into political affairs, but he is one of those who is against Arabs.[83]

Though in an interview with a researcher and AU official Hilal does not engage in the kind of "militantly racist"[84] rhetoric that characterizes genocidal intent, his repetitious casting of a unified Other—al-Nur's Fur—suggests a conception of opposing Arab unity. And in the same speech, he plays off sedentary-nomadic differences, claiming that:

...when the war started many Fur are displaced. But this was not by direct attack. They were scared and left those areas. The movements had built their camps near civilians, so they were scared of attack. Some of these camps were built inside the village. They do this because they are going to take taxes and use children to be armed.

Hilal says that nomads, "his people," in contrast, would never accept life in any camp.[85]

Taken together, that argument; the racial "othering;" his disdain for taxation, settlement, and cowardice; all these integrate myths of nomad and farmer, Arab and African into a single vitriolic picture. The false identities reinforce each other. The idea is all the more powerful because there are elements of truth to Hilal's argument that nomads were wrongly seen to be "importing" violence as a group.

Hilal was a key actor in the Darfur conflict. Widely credited as chief of the Janjaweed, he was first person named on the US State Department's list of persons suspected of war crimes in Darfur. He became the face of the genocide for enormous media and activist campaigns directed at the governments of the United States and Sudan, and the United Nations. It is therefore ironic that one of that campaign's ultimate outputs was resolution 1556, in which the continuity of the nomad-farmer narrative echoes colonial racial narratives—just as it does in Hilal's discourse.

For Mamdani, the resolution and situation around it imply profound problems. "More than anything else," he concludes, "the 'responsibility to protect' is a right to punish but without being held accountable—a clarion call for the recolonization of 'failed' states in Africa."[86] On this basis, he not only rejects the responsibility to protect, but the ICC warrant for Bashir's arrest. And in that context, nomadism, far from being anti-statist, reads as a lynchpin of Sudanese sovereignty. As one analyst noted: "it [was] impossible for the Sudanese government to comply with UN security council resolution 1556—to immediately disarm the Janjawiid—without the government itself surrendering control over Darfur."[87]

This view can easily be misread as apology for the Sudanese government. In light of the alleged crimes, criticism of the resolution can appear morally repugnant. It was relatively rare at the time. But one author, Ali Hagar, presents a fundamental explanation for its rarity: the false nomad-farmer binary. "There is a misapprehension," he writes,

> …that tribal and racial conflicts in Darfur are due to competition over resources between farmers and herdsmen.…There have been more than fifty conferences held in the three Darfur states in the last twenty-five years. More than one hundred research papers, including masters' and doctoral theses, have been written and presented seeking a solution for this problem…to date, all approaches have been insufficient."[88]

Hagar is shrewd. All explanations will remain insufficient so long as they proceed from that initial, simplifying misapprehension. It occurs not only in Darfur, but everywhere nomads are involved in armed conflict.

Nomads and "New Wars"

The Kingdom of Johore is long fallen, but occasionally states and inter-state actors still engage nomads in political dialogue rather than simply securitizing them as the "Other." The process that begins with the distribution of badges to a band of nomads can come to define a regional political situation. One outcome is sedentarization, as for Musa Hilal upon his integration into Khartoum's political elite:

> As the father in his desert tent roof took pride in his independence, so did the son in his lavish, scented villa in Khartoum, hundreds of miles away from

Darfur, take pride in being the government's man 'appointed' by the government to fight the rebels.[89]

At the same time Hilal settles, it should be noted that nomads have themselves been able to draw political interlocutors out of sedentarism, sometimes. In Somalia in 1974, for example, the anthropologist I.M. Lewis reports that urbanized Mogadishites were known to abandon assignments on the government's "Rural Development Campaign" in favor of nomadism because they "found the rigours of the bush more appealing." This was in spite of the drought of the mid-1970s, which saw some 200,000 nomads lose their herds and end up in relief camps. Interestingly in that instance, it was another international interlocutor—the Soviet Union—which funded the subsequent sedentarization process. The Somali government, in exchange, offered formerly nomadic labor for the growing Russian fish canning industry on the coast. As Lewis writes: "this sudden re-location of the Somali population...where they were to change from nomadic herdsmen to sedentary cultivators or fishermen (both occupations traditionally despised by the nomads) was a bold and hazardous undertaking."[90] The Somali state's degeneration in the following decades speaks to just how hazardous it was.

The resulting instability in that case—and many like it—fits neatly into Mary Kaldor's conception of security. Nomadism occupies a vital but unspecified place in her arguments about "new wars." On account of its tendency towards extra-or anti-statism, the practice plays an important role in conflicts which are marked by the breakdown of state activity; of distinctions between the economic, political, civil and military; and of territorial divisions between internal and external.[91] Such are the predominant conflicts of today, Kaldor argues, and further that: "the most common fighting units are paramilitary groups, that is to say, autonomous groups of armed men generally centered around an individual leader...Often, paramilitary groups are associated with particular extremist parties or political factions."[92] This describes nomadic militias the world over. But perhaps more interesting, in the context of her argument, are the ways in which nomadism might make us think more critically about her "new wars" theory.

Kaldor writes that "precisely because the new wars are a social condition that arise as the formal political economy withers, they are vey difficult to end." As we will see in the next chapter, nomadic economies are often by definition "informal," not just in times of conflict. Kaldor continues, "diplomatic negotiations from above fail to take into account the underlying social relations; they treat the various factions as though they were proto-states." Here again, what Kaldor sees as specific to conflict is actually a constant in the relationship between the international community and nomads. Ignoring the political nature of mobility, the international community places nomadism into a proto-state mold of indigenous peoples, sometimes actually allotting them a state within a state, as in the case of American Indian reservations of the indigenous zones of South America. Another idea of Kaldor's is that "temporary ceasefires or truces may merely legitimize new agreements or partnerships that, for the moment, suit the various factions ... as long as the power relations remain the same, sooner or later the violence will start again."[93] This captures not just Hemeti's behavior in the "new war" in Darfur, but nomadic-state agreements in the region back to the Fur Sultanate.

Kaldor's "new wars" are defined by sub-state, transnational, fluid identity politics. These are characteristics of globalization; indeed the subtitle of Kaldor's book runs "organized violence in a global era." But nomadism—a practice that long precedes any articulated concept of globalization—reflects all of these elements in conflict, and continues to do so. This chapter has explored why and how this happens, first in terms of its existential threat to the state, and then its military value, its connection to reconciliation in humanitarian intervention, the creation and prosecution of terrorism, and racial conflict. In each instance, nomadism—usually perceived as an archaic practice—played a key political role in a "new war."

4

ECONOMIES OF MOVEMENT

"She could never see any bad in any Gypsy—a thief was not a thief but, say, someone who divested of his traditional economic niche, had adapted to a new but still symbiotic relationship with the *gadjo*, from whom he earned his goods in exchange for status in a period of economic and political crisis…. She wasn't kidding, nor was she entirely wrong."[1]

From *Bury Me Standing*
Isabel Fonseca, 1995

This chapter explores how nomadism influences the global economy. It begins by considering some of the shortcomings of the journalistic and anthropological literature on mobility before building a nomadic economic perspective on the basis of primary and secondary research on five economic systems which nomadism renders illegible to the state and conventional indicators: i) livestock production; ii) distribution of aid; iii) overland staple and narcotics trading; iv) extractive-industrial investment in educational development; v) and extractive-industrial land acquisition. The chapter then provides examples of actors advocating the dominant economic conceptions in the international arena before concluding with a look at Arun Agrawal's research on the nomadic bartering system of Rajasthan which, like systems i–v, calls into question the assumptions of those dominant conceptions.

THE CIVILIZATION OF PERPETUAL MOVEMENT

A Material Connection

In 1996, *The Washington Post* ran a story describing life among some of the nomadic Tuareg in Mali. It began like this:

> Sididi Ag Inaka has never used a television, toilet or telephone. He has never read a newspaper. He has never heard of a facsimile machine. He has never seen an American dollar. He is entirely disconnected from the global economy and its ever-rippling waves. And he does not care. 'My father was a nomad, his father was a nomad, I am a nomad, my children will be nomads,' said Inaka, who was not sure of his age but looked to be in his fifties. 'This is the life of my ancestors. This is the life that we know. We like it.'[2]

Many of the nomads discussed in this chapter live, like Inaka, in a state of extreme material simplicity. Attention to the realities of subsistence must inform any discussion of nomadic political economy: it is important not to over-determine nomadism; agency is a complicated idea. We shall take up this theoretical problem in chapter six. However the idea that nomads are "disconnected from the global economy" is a misguided assumption, disproven by the examples cited in this chapter. A lack of material possessions does not remove an actor from a system, even if that lack might diminish an actor's influence within the system.

Though the *Post* reporter intimates surprise at Inaka's situation—with the dramatic fragment "and he does not care"—Inaka himself does not seem so surprised. The reporter goes on, in a slightly awestruck mode, to describe what he sees as the ardor and isolation of Inaka's life: total dependence on animals; rejection of bureaucracy, even hospitals; ignorance of the Malian president's name. Journalists are not paid to spend a great deal of time with nomads, and it is not surprising that this one reinforces the notion that nomadism is an isolated and archaic practice. In spite of that, the headline is insightful: "Nomads by Choice."

The choice is key. What appears to be a total separation from the global economy in the reporter's mainstream understanding is actually a managed relationship, inseparable from political action and cultural identity. Again, it is wise to be cautious about the intention of nomads and not over-determine their choices. But examples from the general category indicate that the relationship between nomadism and the global economy is rich, dynamic, and mutually constitutive.

Tourism, Nostalgia, and Superficiality in Economic Mobility Studies

Inaka's West African Sahara is a useful place to start thinking about how exactly that relationship works, partly in light of some recent scholarly work on the region. In the old Eurocentric imagination, nomads in the Sahara conjures up camel caravans, passage under myrrh-scented oasis gates, and the burnt mercantilism of gold carried across trackless sands. But recently, some anthropologists and international technocrats alike have updated their notions of nomadic incorporation into a "globalized economy." Often this takes the form of comment on the juxtaposition of old and new technology in which, for example, photovoltaics on a tent roof are an indicator of prosperity,[3] or

> Suda wears a digital watch from Japan. She drinks green tea from China and owns shoes from Italy. She is 30 years old, has three children, and successfully manages a goat herd in the Algerian Sahara. She is a Kel Ahaggar nomad in the age of globalization.[4]

This description is from Anja Fischer's essay on nomadic connections to global networks, and it suggests something tense about that old/new juxtaposition, and the wider anthropology of mobility. The repetitive sentence structure, the monosyllabic pronoun openings, and the lack of conditional or subordinate clauses all belie the grammatical complexity of the rest of Fischer's essay. The staccato tone of the passage implies confrontation, a conversation with the less sophisticated, as if, perhaps, she were correcting the *Post* reporter. It suggest that the *truth* is very simple. That is: goat herders possess commodities produced around the world.

But what does this actually tell us? It is a relatively well-known phenomenon—high-end purveyors of those commodities often use the juxtaposition of "primitive" peoples and modern technology to send messages about the free market, innovation, and potential wealth acquisition.[5] Fischer's tone suggests a sense of injustice about this material integration of nomads into globalization, but without explanation. In a historical context of sedentary oppression this makes sense; but it is strange to find it in an essay where Fischer is trying to emphasize the economic agency of Saharan nomads—who "certainly [are] not victims but instead play a role in the globalization process."[6] The tension foreshadows a more significant incoherence. Here, for example, Fischer discusses how the nomads "play a role":

The old trade routes the *Imuhar* created are still used today for a subversive international economy. On the other hand, African migrant streams move through the Sahara, using routes frequented and completed by the Imuhar. Thus, the Sahara is still a hub in globalized space.[7]

The first question which arises is whether migrant streams are themselves part of the "subversive international economy." Why does Fischer set up that economy and those streams in opposition to one another? And how is it that their *opposition*—"on the other hand" followed by "thus"— indicates the Sahara as a hub in globalized space? Does the use of an old nomadic migratory route really constitute a contemporary, subversive involvement by nomads in the global economy? The nomads were rarely the sole or even primary beneficiaries of the routes in previous centuries: in the Sahara and elsewhere, colonial traders and other non-subversives took advantage of them too. There is a complex history which is glossed over. And yet Fischer scrabbles to empower nomadism on the basis of this unclear logic about "migratory routes," or frequently, tourism.

It is worth pausing over the latter to recognize the deeply nostalgic relationship between tourism and nomadism. Nostalgia supposes decline. The subsequent tension between tourism and anthropology in a rising global economy is present in the *Post* piece, in Fischer's work, and more broadly in nomad studies.

In his study of Tuaregs working in the tourist sectors of Algeria, Libya, and Mali, Marko Scholze addresses this directly. He argues that, in spite of what he sees as anthropology's negative attitude towards tourism, the behavior of these Tuaregs illustrates how "local populations incorporate foreign cultural elements and come to terms with processes of globalization." He tries to answer the question: "does the engagement of Tuareg in tourism mean that they have abandoned their nomadic traditions?" He provides anthropological data like Tuaregs' references to the Toyota Land Cruiser as the "Japanese Camel," and their appropriation of "new skills" when they start a tourist agency (basic accounting, European cooking). To his credit, he does not suggest that this answers his question. He does conclude, however, that the Tuareg "like other peripatetic peoples, create an economic niche of their own that relies on specialized spatial mobility and their cultural exoticism as their main assets in the tourism business."[8]

Though Scholze digs deeper, his analysis is similar to Fischer's (it is also in the same volume) in that it describes nomadic business as a "niche" carved out of the dominant market and state. The title, "Between the Worlds" suggests how exotic the whole situation remains, even in the context of an imagined, homogenous "tourism business." Fundamentally, he does not look at how nomadism builds political economy—he looks at how it survives within one that already exists. "In tapping a global resource," he concludes, "at least some of the actors have become both rich and politically influential [but]…the owners of a local travel agency have not become global players."[9]

But not being a "global player" does not mean the Tuareg are "between worlds." And, in fact, some of them are "global players" on his terms—if he means actors whose political-economic influence is recognized internationally. Scholze actually mentions an interesting example in the person of Mano Dayak, whom he identifies as "the most prominent actor" in the early days of Tuareg tourist agencies and also a political leader of the trans-national Tuareg rebellion in the early 1990s.

Understanding how someone like Dayak's nomadic identity relates to and defines the global economy requires more than under-specified examples of nomadism's "migratory routes," or shallow examples like Suda and her watch. Nomads remain economically relevant in ways beyond capitalization on nostalgia for adventure tourists, and there are in fact quantitative studies illustrating nomadism's influence on the global economy.

Illegible Nomadic Livestock Production

One highly sophisticated study that deals with this relationship is Peter Little's *Somalia: Economy Without State*. It focuses on the cross-border livestock trade between Somalia and Kenya to understand the realities of what he calls a "stateless economy" in the late 1990s. The relative success and, in some sectors, growth of the Somali economy, he writes, "challenges many social science notions about economy, governance, and institutions…" The situation was striking, and remains so. There was no ministry of finance, there was no central bank, there were virtually no formal institutions providing financial services—but currency remained in circulation, and transaction costs remained low.

One of the essential explanations he posits for this is that "Somali resiliency has been enhanced by its strong dependence on nomadic pastoralism, a livelihood well adapted to stateless circumstances but brutally defensive when threatened…"[10] Little comes out of a tradition of thinking on "informal"—without official regulation—economies, which has focused especially on sub-Saharan Africa. The most obvious relation between nomadism and "informality" concerns borders. In Somalia, "it is not uncommon for Somali herders to cross the border and graze their animals in Northeastern Kenya during rainy months." This movement has occurred in both directions, since before Somalia's "statelessness" began in 1991. It continues today.[11]

In such a vein it is easy to understand how nomadism is suited to a stateless economy. Aside from not paying any taxes, the nomadic pastoralist is freed from the states' recurrent attempts to undermine his livelihood—like Somalia's repeated resettlement schemes, irrigation investments, and subsidization of elite traders between 1961 and 1991. Little and others have noted that some pastoralists actually benefited from what the rest of the world referred to as a "failed state." Fewer of their cattle died, in the droughts of the 1990s, then did those of their Kenyan neighbors to the immediate South; the statistics Little gathers on the livestock trade show a spectacular growth during this period of deregulation.[12] He is careful not to paint a rosy picture of Somali life in the period he studies, even as he deploys such examples. But corroborating the previous chapter, he notes that the nomadic population was suited not only to the statelessness of Somalia but its violence. But their mobility often allowed them to escape the militias that savaged the sedentary and urban populations.

The maintenance of the livestock economy in Somalia in the face of such adversity has implications worldwide. Especially in the context of recent growth in demand for meat—driven most noticeably by China, India, and Brazil—nomadically produced livestock constitutes a significant supply—one sixth by value of world exports, for example, coming just from pastoral East Africa, and much of that from Somalia. Other livestock products play a role as well. The global camel milk market alone is valued at $10 billion. Cashmere, leather, and manure also make significant contributions to many states' GDPs.[13]

Despite that value, working out those numbers is an extremely difficult task. This is often a function of state information-collecting methodologies favoring those practices—sedentary rather than nomadic—which are, in Scott's terminology, most easily made legible. Scholars who try to work out the statistics lack reliable data. In an article[14] proposing a new, tailored Total Economic Value (TEV) framework for analyzing nomadic pastoralism in East Africa, Hesse and MacGregor note, for instance, that "there are no reliable data on pastoral population numbers in East Africa since national census figures do not disaggregate by ethnic group or livelihood." They continue:

> A significant but unknown proportion of the pastoral economy does not pass through official markets but occurs within the community, while the economic returns on pastoral labour are unknown as *the majority of pastoralists do not draw salaries nor pay income tax* ... In practice, a lot of data in East Africa are the result of a series of assumptions, imperfections, estimates and best guesses by a range of actors involved with statistical collection, collation and analysis... This is often because *data is collected primarily for other reasons such as raising tax revenue or directing extension services.*[15]

Mobility as a modern state evasion technique is apparent here, and has direct relevance to East Africa's economy. Hesse and MacGregor do not dwell on it. Instead, they work towards a methodology able to account for nomadic pastoralism's contribution to the agricultural GDP of three countries. The methodology is ingenious, based on proxy indicators and inferences like this one: "official figures indicate a very high proportion of indigenous cattle in the national herds (75–97%), and given that such animals are predominantly reared by pastoral and agro-pastoral communities, it is reasonable to infer from these figures that pastoralism is a major contributor rather than dairying or ranching."[16]

Through such deductions, Hesse and MacGregor demonstrate repeatedly—for the beef, hide, and milk economies in Kenya, Uganda, and Tanzania—that nomadic pastoralism plays a significant role in subsistence, trade, and raw material inputs.[17] In their TEV framework, these are "direct values." Hesse and MacGregor go on to demonstrate "indirect values"—nomads as brands for tourist operators, or as manure producers for farmers, for example. They do not, however, pursue the two final values of the emergent TEV framework: option value, which refers to the future flow of costs and benefits; and existence values, which they describe as "values that are held by global society for the persistence of an entity or activity."

The concept of "existence value," while it has explanatory power, has not developed enough ideological force to significantly influence state decision-making. It is therefore of little use to Hesse and MacGregor, given what they see as their central challenge:

> For policy makers, a key question is whether pastoralism offers the most cost-effective investment for the drylands of East Africa, particularly in a context

of increasing climate variability because of global climate change. The challenge is to provide the evidence to convince government that it does.[18]

This is a formidable objective—and in sectors other than livestock, nomadic advocacy faces even greater resistance.

Illegible Nomadic Distribution of Foreign Aid

Another way to think about the international economics of nomadism is with regard to foreign investment and aid as drivers. In Mali, for example—just as in Kenya, Uganda, and Tanzania:

> …administrators are reluctant to recognize pastoral ownership of this disparate pastoral space. They cannot measure it, nor circumscribe it with lines on a map. Yet this is where we find Mali's livestock economy, following a production cycle which is in harmony with its natural resource base, unless drought or violence disturb the balance.[19]

This is from a 1998 UN report co-authored by Ibrahim ag Youssef, a Tuareg analyst who identifies himself as a nomad.[20] Youssef's report concerns disarmament in the early 1990s, but it clearly recalls Hesse and MacGregor's livestock analysis from across the continent. Throughout it is clear that when the "balance" he describes is disrupted by violence or drought, "nomadic space" remains important to the economy as a whole, not just livestock production.

"A Targui's[21] space," Youssef writes, "is composed of a series of complementary points, places where he can find the elements he needs for his animals." These "points" range from common grazing lands along a river to shifting sites of commercial interactions with sedentary farmers. Abstract "nomadic space" dictates local resource distribution like a highway dictates traffic flow; it thus encloses the introduction of foreign capital.

The experiences of one agricultural engineer vividly illustrate the point, and connect it to a larger international donor economy. In 1994, during the most violent months of the rebellion, the militant Tuareg group Front Populaire de Libération de l'Azawad (FPLA, a pre-cursor to today's MNLA), had driven all Malian administrators—and thus their development projects and economic influence—from the rural areas. But the engineer in question, Cheik Abdoulaye Bathily, continued to live in the northern village of Hama Kougali. With funds from the UN's World Food Program (WFP), he was working with villagers to construct a fifty-hectare cement perimeter which would have significant consequences for the immediate area and also for the capital, Bamako, which is mostly fed on imported cereals. He was allowed to remain working when all other technocrats were forced to flee because his project accounted for conceptions of property-ownership and space that fit into more nomadic, less state-centric ideas of the local population.[22] The lands around Hama Kougali, he realized, had been "jointly owned" by the sedentary and nomadic populations, and this ownership extended to the town of Tin Aouker. In his project, therefore, every time the villagers he worked with collected WFP food and supplies for the perimeter for Hama Kougali, some of it went to Tin Aouker and the lands and people in between. The project was not strictly localized according to the state or INGO's administrative boundaries or conceptions of property. As a result, the FPLA population around Tin Aouker called for his safety. And the key point is that the sedentary villagers of Hama Kougali believed that this was not only part of the common interest, but also appropriate. They saw it not as extortion by an armed, nomadic group, but the way the economy should work. Bathily was thus doubly protected, and his understanding of the spectrum of nomadism ensured the flow of international aid as an economic driver.

Bathily was operating in the context of a very dramatic anti-state nomadism—armed elements of the FPLA. But his project's sensitivity to nomadism and its subsequent success illustrate, just as Hesse and MacGregor's study did, a more general political-economic point. As Davies and Hatfield argue:

> Despite a growing body of evidence that highlights the economic and environmental importance of pastoralism, few governments are ready to tolerate mobile livestock production and many pursue explicit or inadvertent policies of settlement.[23]

The reason, as we have seen, is that nomadism is often an anti-state practice. To understand the ways in which nomadism interacts with the global economy, the indicators states do not collect must be identified and analyzed in detail.

Nomadic Identity of Trade Routes

One anthropologist who is extremely acute in this regard is Judith Scheele. In her book *Smugglers and Saints of the Sahara*, she uses her immersive experiences in the Western Sahara to re-conceptualize trade, regional exchange, and mobility. "Throughout the region," she writes, "debates over morality and concepts of civilisation, rather than, say, economic viability or legal status, continue to underpin local classifications of trade."[24] Scheele is contributing to the "anarchist history"[25] of the globe that James Scott hoped for, but focusing on the Sahara instead of Southeast Asia. For Scheele, the Sahara is a vibrant, non-state center rather than a marginal zone.

And just as in Scott's analysis, nomadism is a key practice for the population she studies. She even has identified a town—if it can be called that, she repeatedly problematizes[26] the term—that can actually be defined by nomadism. Moreover, she has identified it in the present day. Where Scott sees his "anarchist zone" disappearing before the onslaught of space conquering state technologies, Scheele sees al-Khalil "bearing all the trappings of 'modernity'" even as it signifies continuity with pre- and extra-state social organizations of the "fabled trading towns of Timbuktu in northern Mali or Ghadames in contemporary Libya." "Khalilis," she learned in her sixteen-month residence around the town, "like to stress continuity over change." She writes from her discussion with them, and her observations in the region, that

> al-Khalil's intrinsic and very visible outside dependency, as well as its brutal cosmopolitanism, fake autonomy, immorality and adaptability to change… force us to question preconceived notions about Saharan settlement, exchange and regional unity, and to develop a new conceptual framework that can grasp it not as an exception, but as an indicator of lasting features of Saharan life.

"True Khalilis," concludes Scheele, "are always on the move, and al-Khalil is never the same two days in a row."[27]

What, really, does this mean? Al-Khalil is a trading post that caters to the overland Algerian-Malian commerce that, according to Scheele, has been essentially outlawed since Algerian independence in 1962. The pastoralist Tuareg who trade their livestock against staples like pasta, petrol and cigarettes are the most obvious nomadic presence, and are an obvious cipher for the continuity of regional trade. Historically this population exploited, guided and preyed upon trans-Saharan, Atlantic-Mediterranean-Sudanese trade routes. They did not, and do not, view states dividing up the Sahara as allies in their trade. Another anecdote from Youssef's 1998 disarmament report provides a Malian example for why this is the case.

It used to be said in the North that no Targui herdsman would venture into the bush without his water-bottle, his green tea, and his 10,000 Fcfa note (worth $20 these days, but twice as much before the January 1994 devaluation). If the herdsman heard the sound of a Landrover engine, his hand would dive immediately to the bottom of his chest pocket, and bring forth the 10,000 francs. If he was lucky, the government official would just lean out the window and take the money.[28]

Following the March 1991 Malian revolution, this relationship had straightforward security consequences that Youssef explores—the Targui sought retribution. In the context of Scheele's work on the area, the story belies a more complicated relationship than simple exploitation, or nomadic state evasion to protect resources from "tax." Scheele cites a petition,[29] sent by one Ḥammu Zafzaf to the Malian Government "on behalf of the 'traders of Kidal' against the imposition of customs duties and the subsequent confiscation of trade goods." This petition, by Algerian traders to the Malian government, is a good example of transnational sedentary action motivated by sedentary-nomadic relations. As Scheele argues, it "shows the close interaction between Algerian traders and local nomadic populations who imported goods from the Touat, their mutual interdependence, the predominance of regional trade, and the importance of credit extended to nomads."

The petition was sent in 1962, but Scheele's work itself provides us with evidence of a "mutual interdependence" of nomads and traders today. After criss-crossing the region in a truck carrying dates, she writes this:

> Truck trading is based on and creates its own social networks, which include families and local religious dignitaries as well as custom officials and traders on both ends and along the way; a hierarchy that might be at odds with Algerian official conceptions of value, but is, in northern Mali, understood to be central to local society. Ighles and his companions define themselves not as traders, and even less as employees, but rather, albeit with a slight ironic smile, as 'nomads', *ruḥḥul*.[30]

The political and cultural economies of citizens within the Algerian and Malian states are dependent on the trade of men like Ighles, who were transporting not only dates but messages, petrol, a rotating cast of preachers, displaced family members, and migrant workers. The social networks and inherited knowledge that make this trade possible are concrete examples of how the cloudy nomadic "migratory routes" affect contemporary trade. The nomadic identity is ultimately more important than the "route."

This nomadic identity bears on global, not just regional, commerce. It has direct relevance, for example, to the international narcotics economy. The UN Office of Drugs and Crime identifies the Sahara region as a center of drug trafficking,[31] and hundreds of millions of dollars have been spent by a variety of governments in an effort to curtail this economy. The United States has dedicated anti-drug trafficking operations in the region, under the umbrella of its $500 million Operation Enduring Freedom—Trans Sahara. One way to explain the persistence[32] of the narcotics economy in the face of these vast opposing resources is by thinking about the nomadic truckers.

> [The] intimate connection of truck trade with local categories of value and socially approved trans-border connections explains why…from a local point of view at least, there is no doubt that the slow and meandering rhythm of truck travel, although trucks are quite as much involved in carrying smuggled goods as other means of transport, is morally sound.[33]

Following this logic, the moral integrity of the trade in local opinion—and thus its security—is in part guaranteed by the category "nomad," even if, for example, moving drugs could be considered *haram* (forbidden) in local Islamic discourse. This is why the quantity of cocaine which arrives annually for processing in Guinea, for example, is contingent on truckers' nomadic self-definition—"they pride themselves on their sense of direction and their gallantry, which sets them apart from Malian or 'black' drivers."[34] What, and how much, is traded depends upon who is allowed to trade it. The market thus fluctuates on the basis of trader identities in addition to supply and demand.[35]

Self-definition, of course, does not alone make a nomad. Is truck driving essential to Ighles' culture? Is it a political behavior? All of Scheele's research suggests that it is. Even if the truckers are slightly ironic about what they call themselves, they ultimately take the category seriously, and have a high degree of agency that further supports the notion of nomadism as a political-cultural choice. "They spend more time on the road than 'back home'…not only due to their exploitation by ruthless businessmen, but rather to their own taste: even where cities are within reach, they prefer to sleep out in the *badiya*…."[36]

These truckers and pastoralists are key citizens of al-Khalil. It is not a state, or a town, but it is more than a truckstop. Stalls where the traders and drivers and pastoralists shelter and work might move anytime. The community's existence is predicated on that ability. Conceptually, it is not a place well provided for by international relations theory, the UN, Mali or Algeria. Its citizens respect no borders, but remain crucial to the regional and global economies. Finally they not only "evade" state systems, they frequently appropriate and re-sculpt what they find attractive about those systems. The "growing feeling of loss of autonomy," Scheele writes at the end of her book, "is mostly met with ever more outrageous and self-glorifying boasts: nobody, people say, will ever be able to rule the 'democratic and popular Republic of al-Khalil'..." The nomads articulate a republic of their own—a republic without borders. It is a place with a real GDP and modern diversity of trade, but beyond the control of conventionally dominant actors, like cartel operating "Colombians" or America's imagined "Islamic terrorists," as the truckers put it. Such people, in Scheele's Khalili ventriloquism, "will have to marry local Tuareg wives, and then they will soon learn how to keep quiet..." The ultimate strategy, of course, is the most fundamentally nomadic, and not contingent upon particularly Tuareg identity: "at the very worst, Khalilis will pick up their goods, water tanks and satellite phones, and simply move somewhere else."[37]

Nomadism and MNC Relations: Development

Not all nomads are able to execute their practices so effectively, or are the beneficiaries of equally kind historical circumstance. Away from the center of such a regional overland network, nomadism is less influential economically. Once again it is evident that the influence cannot be understood from a purely "economic" perspective. In the Gobi Desert, on the border of Mongolia and China, mining executives and nomads have recently been learning this lesson (and not) from each other.

The post Cold-War period has seen an explosion in the extraction of mineral resources in Mongolia. The most substantial deposits are located in the southeastern part of the country, in the migratory cycle of a population of nomadic pastoralists. The most significant extraction operation to date is the Oyu Tolgoi (OT) copper and gold mine, claimed to be the world's largest, which is located eighty kilometers north of China—the state with the highest demand for copper in the world. Analysts predict profit from the mine will ultimately account for some thirty percent of Mongolia's GDP and that as a result, "Mongolia has a chance of becoming a Qatar or a Brunei: a country that has only a small population but almost all of it, in global terms, loaded."[38]

Construction of the mine and supporting infrastructure represent a $6 billion investment by the Canadian firm Ivanhoe and the Anglo-Australian multinational corporation (MNC) Rio Tinto, which now owns a 49 per cent controlling stake in the project. Rio Tinto is a publicly traded company listed on the London Stock Exchange and the Australian Securities Exchange, and one of the largest and most profitable MNCs in existence—in 2011 it posted revenues of $56.57 billion, and *Fortune* listed it as the one hundred and fortieth largest company in the world.[39]

Rio Tinto has come under scrutiny for the environmental and human rights consequences of its operations several times. In 2008 the Finance Ministry of Norway ejected Rio Tinto from its sovereign wealth fund portfolio on the basis of what the Finance Minister called "our unwillingness to run an unacceptable risk of contributing to grossly unethical conduct." She continued, "the Council on Ethics has concluded that Rio Tinto is directly involved, through its participation in the Grasberg mine in Indonesia, in the severe environmental damage caused by that mining operation."[40] Other reports[41] at the time accused Rio Tinto of complicity in attendant human rights abuses. Rio Tinto, however, emphasizes its compliance with international regulation and devotion to principles of sustainable development. Nonetheless, NGOs and nomadic representatives in Mongolia accuse Rio Tinto and OT of destroying nomadic livelihoods in the Gobi.[42]

The Norwegian ejection was the result of a complex interaction between local actors, NGOs, MNCs, and national governments. Theoretically, the emergence of Indigenous Peoples IP—Human Rights discourse pressures MNCs into pursuing development of local communities in addition to profit. In this context, the nomads of the Gobi have much in common with the populations around Indonesia's Grasberg mine, or other peoples similarly affected by extractive industry. However, nomadism distinguishes the Gobi population and others like it from sedentary populations in some important ways—usually to their detriment, rather than, as in the Sahara, their benefit. The common "nomadic" argument about mining in the Gobi runs like this:

> From what I'm led to believe, there really aren't that many herders in the region of the mines. The Gobi is vast, and very sparse. The handful of herders that may reside in the region isn't of huge significance, especially when you compare it to oil & gas ventures in other parts of the world that border on civilisation. *The traditional Mongolian herder is by nature nomadic, so in the event of any water shortage in the area it's likely they'll stroll off to greener pastures.*[43]

This idea fundamentally misunderstands nomadism by assuming that the ability to move and the absence of formal boundaries reduces a population's connection to given land. This passage comes from a Perth-based blog, but was prevalent among the journalists covering OT in the fall of 2011 at a ceremony marking the halfway point of mine construction.[44]

Around that occasion, Rio Tinto and OT hosted a three-day tour for journalists, senior executives, and Mongolian politicians. The tour program emphasized OT's stated commitment to sustainable development as outlined in the guidelines of the Organization for Economic Cooperation and Development (OECD) and elsewhere. Company representatives repeatedly highlighted OT's substantial spending on local communities in terms of environmental and social impact assessments, hospitals, and funding scholarships, to take three examples. The following, from OT CEO Cameron McRae, is representative:

> Oyu Tolgoi offers an unrivalled opportunity which will be shared by all the citizens of Mongolia for decades to come....Over the next five years we're spending US$85 million—114 bn tugriks—on it. And we've established a graduate scholarship programme for 120 students at Mongolian universities and 30 Mongolian students at international universities....[45]

McRae provided other, equally dramatic examples of Oyu Tolgoi's benevolence. But sustained attention to flows of capital he mentions illustrates some of the problems with integrating nomadism into corporate social responsibility (CSR) initiatives.

Many of the scholarships that OT funds, for example, are awarded by the Zorig Foundation. This NGO is prominently located across the street from Ulaanbaatar's Sukhbataar square, in the former embassy of Yugoslavia, and is well respected. The executive director of the foundation credibly claims to have rebuffed attempts by elites to bribe him in exchange for selecting their children for the scholarship. What is more troubling to him than those incidents, he says, is that the OT scholarships are exclusively devoted to hard sciences useful in resource extraction.[46] That is, devoted to training future employees of OT, or if not OT itself, then the mining industry. This suggests dependency theory's mono-industrial replication[47] and trans-national elite alliance, though it is portrayed as development.

Per Rio Tinto's development guidelines,[48] OT emphasizes that scholarships are open to, and even target, the nomadic population as well as the elite. The reality is more complicated. Only three of thirty regional sample *gers* (better known as yurts), for example, contained pamphlets from OT listing such scholarships. One of these nomadic families' relationship to the pamphlets illustrates the chronic difficulties facing such a scholarship program. The family used the pamphlets as fuel for the stove and the sturdy tote bags they arrived in for storage. One young woman who had read a pamphlet complained that she had read it too late to take advantage of it for her son. She blamed herself for the oversight, but like many other nomadic herders, she linked her inability to attend meetings with OT representatives to her family's frequent movements. The consequent lack of relationship, she believed, would have thwarted her efforts even if she had read the pamphlet in time.[49]

Nomadism and MNC Relations: Land Acquisition and FPIC

For that woman and others, the possibility of competing for a scholarship from OT did not make up for the perceived injustices the company had perpetrated—the most fundamental of which was the acquisition of land without free and prior informed consent (FPIC). FPIC "is a specific right for Indigenous Peoples as recognised in the United Nations Declaration on the Rights of Indigenous Peoples (UNDRIP)"[50] under which:

> States shall consult and cooperate in good faith with the Indigenous Peoples concerned through their own representative institutions in order to obtain FREE, PRIOR and INFORMED CONSENT prior to approval of any project affecting their land or territories.[51]

Mongolia is signatory to UNDRIP; and according to Rio Tinto's published "Community Standards":

> [Rio Tinto's] position is that it conforms to free prior informed consultation, recognising that there are definitional problems with the word 'consent' and that many countries reserve ultimate decisions on developmental permitting to the sovereign state.[52]

Without exception among the sample of thirty households, the nomads of the Gobi denied that they had been consulted in any meaningful way about the development of Oyu Tolgoi. They often accepted this state of affairs fatalistically, reserving their anger for subsequent broken promises. As another nomadic woman described the development:

> We did know, but only after the decision was made. Oyu Tolgoi always can say they gave us something. The diesel generator in Hanbogd. But they give us old bad things. It breaks and they don't fix it.[53]

Representatives of Rio Tinto and OT, of course, insist that this is not the case.[54] Moreover, according to their conception of private property,[55] consulting the whole nomadic population of the Gobi was unnecessary.[56] In fact, officially, Rio Tinto asserts that it is in full compliance with norms governing treatment of indigenous peoples.[57]

Individual Rio Tinto/OT employees, however, tend to express a more nuanced view. Oyu Tolgoi is one of the most attractive employers in Mongolia—competition for jobs is fierce, and the staff tends to be intelligent, wealthy, well connected, and highly-educated. Often, staff-members have studied in foreign development or politics programs.

Nadmid, for example, was in her early thirties and worked in Oyu Tolgoi's community relations department. A Mongolian citizen with a degree in development studies from North Carolina's Chapel Hill University, Nadmid had returned to Mongolia, in spite of lucrative opportunities abroad, to work towards sustainable development and the preservation of cultural heritage in her own country. Oyu Tolgoi not only provided her the opportunity to do this, she believed, but renumerated her as well as any company in Mongolia could. While she acknowledged the skepticism in the NGO community about the efficacy of OT's community relations program *viz.* "greenwashing," she said she was operating in good faith and suggested that this had not been the case for the smaller community relations team which had existed under the stewardship of Ivanhoe Inc., before Rio Tinto had bought a controlling share in the mine. That team, she said, had been concerned "mostly with charity donations." As far as she was concerned, Ivanhoe's chairman, Robert Friedland, deserved his unfortunate nickname: "Toxic Bob."[58] She said that Oyu Tolgoi was a significant improvement on Ivanhoe.

The story she ultimately told about FPIC, however, was one of frustration. It concerns the construction of roads for the mine, and illustrates the realities of economic investment in FPIC and similar CSR initiatives for nomads.

Driving south from Ulaanbaatar, a traveller must follow hundreds of kilometers of shallow, rough track. Approaching the mining site, this suddenly changes to graded dirt road (or "hardpack") and then pavement. Along the hardpack roads are vast "borrow" pits, where the earth used in the packing and grading has been dug up. Part of Nadmid and the community relation team's job was to conduct a social impact analysis prior to construction of the roads. With regard to the pits, this was very simple. Since there was no property ownership defined locally, Nadmid was mandated to travel the affected area, interviewing nomads, asking if there was anywhere in particular that must not be dug up. What were the hills that were most important for their animals? Were there any areas of particular cultural significance? Nadmid sat in their *gers*, drinking tea, taking notes, making promises. After she completed research about a particular area, she wrote up a report. She then submitted it to her immediate superiors in the community relations department and also to the area construction teams.

While she was interviewing, she said, the construction team made contact with the local mayors and *sum* (district) governors. This bureaucracy immediately approved requests for construction permits. Nadmid volunteered three reasons the local official might have behaved this way—they might have been "impressed by the foreigners"; they might have been bribed; or they might simply not have been paying very much attention. Other reasons are easy to imagine. In any case, the construction team, legitimized by the local government, dug pits for the hardpack in several of the places the nomads asked Nadmid to protect.

Nadmid had highlighted these locations in her report. When she realized what was happening, she went to the construction sites to confront the managers about digging up the flagged areas. The managers, however, showed her authorization from the government. "And anyway," Nadmid concluded, "I'm a youngish local national woman, they barely listen to me."[59] This series of events was a particularly frustrating for Nadmid when, not long after, she had to re-interview some of the same nomads for another construction project.[60] Understandably, they were less inclined to trust her. Some were furious with her. Others, she allowed, understood that she was trying to work on their behalf but that she was over-ruled. And she, of course, understood that if decision-makers at Oyu Tolgoi or Rio Tinto wanted to, they could delegate greater authority to the community relations department and prevent incidents like the one she had described. But they would not, and she would not move companies. The other mining firms she might work for, she said, were "much worse" than Rio Tinto and OT. Other employees expressed similar views. In so far as Rio Tinto dedicates resources to community relations at all, the nomads of the Gobi, like other indigenous groups, have driven the re-allocation of capital through a normative discourse about sustainable development and human rights. However, as we have seen, direct positive consequences have been limited by the poor incorporation of nomadism into corporate social responsibility initiatives.

Nomadism vs Dominant Conceptions of Economic Development

The limited gains are not simply a function of the interaction between nomadism, OT's land acquisition program, and imperfect development programs. Beneath the effect of nomadism on corporate social responsibility—and vice versa—are deeper questions about nomadism's relation to growing states, like Mongolia, dedicated to liberalized trade, private enterprise, and the opening of its markets and resources.[61]

There is no doubt that OT benefits the Mongolian economy in terms of all the conventional indicators. As McRae put it, also on the occasion of the OT halfway ceremony:

> There are also substantial long-lasting practical benefits. We're building significant transport links, including an international-standard airport here at Oyu Tolgoi, and a new road that will link the mine site and Gashuun Sukhait, our border entry point to China....over $700M has been spent with over 1,000 Mongolian suppliers. Five of the major OT construction projects underway in the South Gobi are 100 per cent managed by Mongolian contractors.[62]

This bounty is extremely appealing from a state and moreover, a transnational perspective. But it is less appealing from a nomadic perspective. An analysis of American diplomatic cables on the topic reveals a telling intersection of these views.

In the summer of 2009, Speaker of the American House of Representatives John Boehner and several other US congressmen[63] visited Mongolia. According to a US embassy report,

> CODEL Boehner's first stop was to review the economic challenges faced by a traditional herder family located about 30 miles southwest of the capital Ulaanbaatar and to discuss ways that USAID assistance had aided the family's livestock enterprise. The family of eight shared how the current economic crisis had affected their nomadic lifestyle including cattle, sheep, and goat herding, milking horses, and cheese production. The family also shared how business skills training provided by CHF International and funded by USAID had improved its standard of living. The delegation also reviewed traditional handicrafts and spoke to the craftsman about their economic challenges and how USAID-funded assistance is benefiting them.[64]

The review of what might be called a "show family" for visiting donors and VIPs is common practice among MNCs, and NGOs. The "show family" on the OT program was patently unrepresentative of the local population. That aside, the relentless self-congratulation of the report suggests the breadth of imagination at work. US diplomats slot nomadic herders into a particular conception of what makes for a successful economy, and the Mongolian state does likewise. Attention to the "traditional" satisfies normative requirements, while the "modern" actors form alliances to protect their economic interests. Boehner and his entourage, as subsequent cables make clear, are not primarily concerned with USAID:

> Upon return to Ulaanbaatar, the CODEL joined leading American business people (including representatives from Peabody Energy and Ivanhoe Mines) and one Mongolian who owns a political survey and polling business for dinner at Khan Bank, Mongolia's leading financial institution. The subject on everyone's mind was the likelihood of Parliament accepting the latest terms for the world class Oyu Tolgoi (OT) copper-gold mine investment agreement....[65]

These groups of state representatives and businesspeople are not, of course, monolithic, but they tend to be unified and pro-mining: the US has an advocacy relationship with Mongolia on behalf of Rio Tinto and other MNCs.[66] Rio Tinto was unable to develop OT until October 6th, 2009, when the Mongolian government passed the necessary legislation.

The nomadic community in the Gobi is not monolithic either—but it tends towards a unified anti-mining stance.[67] And between these two clearly opposed camps, there is an obvious discrepancy in power. The more interesting discrepancy, however, is conceptual. Sedentary advocates of the mining take for granted the benefits of "development" that a project like OT entails. They are often very proud. On the final evening of the OT junket, the former president of Mongolia, Natsagiin Bagabandi, gave a speech congratulating the company on reaching the halfway mark. The speech was over dinner in what OT executives affectionately called the "big *ger*"—an oversized model of a nomadic shelter in which they entertained. To much laughter and applause, President Bagabandi concluded his remarks like this:

"I hope that for completion, we can celebrate in a big *house*, not a big *ger*."

While both Bagabandi and the Rio Tinto regime were eager to express their respect for, and even solidarity with, the nomads, the frequency of comments like that indicated a subtext. The ex-President's aside implied that nomadism was primitive and sedentarization represented progress. Given the discourse around the "traditional," this can be interpreted less a function of blunt prejudice than one of entrenched notions about progress that are tied to mainstream theories of free market economics.

The Nomadic Barter Economy

One crucial assumption of those theories is that the barter system is somehow "primitive" compared with an exchange of commodities. Some nomads still barter, and this contributes to perceptions of primitiveness. And not just among ex-Presidents like Bagabandi. In the academy, the economic literature has, according to Arun Agrawal, "taken the difference between barter and commodity exchange as obvious, using as the criterion whether money as a numeraire is involved. This literature has sought," he writes, "to demonstrate the inferiority of barter to monetary exchanges."[68]

But alternative interpretations exist. Agrawal draws attention to a particular nomadic economy in order to question the validity of that barter system inferiority. He focuses on the Raikas of western India, a highly mobile group of nomadic pastoralists. His time with them led him to conclude that "it seems to make no sense to insist on separating barter from commodity exchange. The fact that they seem willing to shift between money and grain for the droppings of their sheep, and that these exchanges are located in a wider political economy that is thoroughly imbued with the influence of money, suggest the pointlessness of such an argument."[69]

This is his starting point for a chapter drawing upon the significant literature documenting the effect of social and political influences on economic outcomes (Berry, Bates, Bhaduri, Sen, etc.). In his analysis of the manure/grain trade between Raikas and farmers, Agrawal observes Raika negotiating sessions along their nomadic route. Conducting a regression on his statistical analysis of price variation, Agrawal finds that the factors most commonly understood to determine price—supply and demand—are insufficient explanation for the Raika economy. His study highlights the influence and variety of sociopolitical factors that set market conditions.

It also highlights a point nomadism teaches about economics generally, contra Bagabandi: "The importance of context becomes starkly obvious in the case of the Raikas precisely because there is substantial variation from one negotiating situation to another." From this, Agrawal builds a grander theoretical claim: that his study "allows us to explore the significance of social and political influences on prices."[70] For our purposes it can be noted simply that the nomadism which increases variation in such a model is of no less inherent value or relevance to the Indian—and thus global—economy than the sedentarism which might decrease such variation.

Nomads often operate on this basis, and as we have seen in this chapter, they exert significant, complex influence on the global economy. Nomadism drives development investment from Rio Tinto but that investment is ineffective because it does not understand or take seriously mobility; this lack of understanding also characterizes academic and regulatory thinking on nomadic trade in the Sahara. The economic future of the Raikas, like the East African Pastoralists, the Saharan FPLA, Scheele's truckers, and the nomads of the Gobi will continue to tread between integration and escape from the state and interstate system. Each of these groups remains critical to the economic life of its region, even if their respective practices are sometimes illegible to conventional measurements of states.

5

THE CLIMATE OF THE COMMONS

"A cloud gathers, the rain falls, men live; the cloud disperses without rain, and men and animals die."

from *Arabian Sands*
Wilfred Thesiger, 1959

This chapter explores some of the relationships between nomadism, conservation, and climate change. It begins by addressing Hardin's "tragedy of the commons" and its dominance in discussions of nomadism and the environment in international relations and the media. The chapter then explores the nomadic causes and consequences of that dominance through five related phenomena: i) policies on nomads which contribute to the environmental problems they are meant to alleviate; ii) instrumentalization of Hardinesque arguments for security and economic purposes iii) joint nomad—state "community conservation" projects iv) international NGO advocacy for nomads and v) nomadic resistance to numbers i) through iii). The chapter examines these processes in India, China, Tanzania, and Mongolia, but draws on examples from around the world. It concludes with an assessment of the normative value of international non-governmental organizations (INGOs) dedicated to nomads.

Nomadism and "The Tragedy of the Commons"

The environmental arguments about pastoral nomadism have significant implications. As R.B. Harris argues in the *Journal of Arid Environments*, "livestock grazing is [the] dominant form of land use in arid biomes worldwide."[1] And rangeland degradation—the environmental problem most associated with arid biomes—is not only a problem for nomadic pastoralists. It results in "hydrological disturbances, dust storms, commodity scarcity" and a variety of other dangerous phenomenon. The rangelands of the Qinghai-Tibetan Plateau (QTP) alone "are located in the source area for most of Asia's major rivers, upstream and upwind of upwards of 40% of the world's human population." Recent disasters in Asia linked to rangeland degradation have included repeated dust storms in Eastern China; the drying of the Yellow River; and the Yangtze River floods—which cost billions of dollars and thousands of lives.[2]

Traditionally, causal arguments about pastoral nomadism in these processes fall into one of two camps. One holds that it is a sustainable practice, the other that it degrades rangelands to non-utility and hazardous instability. The theoretical starting point for the debate—straw man for the first camp and pillar for the second—is Garret Hardin's 1968 essay "The Tragedy of the Commons." Hardin's essential point, here summarized by McCay and Acheson, is this:

> A herdsman puts his animals on a pasture that he uses in common with other herdsmen. Even though there are signs that the condition of the pasture will worsen with additional stocking, it is only rational for each herdsman to add more animals to his herd because he gains the full benefits of each additional animal while sharing the costs of overgrazing with the other herdsmen. The positive utility to the individual herdsman of adding an extra animal is + 1; the negative utility is but a fraction of-1.[3]

It follows that a population of rational pastoral nomads would eventually overgraze any common to destruction. This meshes neatly with depoliticizing conceptions of nomads as forces of nature, consuming a landscape (or indeed raiding a settlement) to nil before moving on. It also implies near total ignorance of both economics and rangeland ecology.

Though mainstream international relations rarely addresses nomadism directly, when it addresses climate change it often draws on Hardin's argument. In the introduction to their 2007 work *International Relations and Global Climate Change*, Luterbacher and Sprinz write that "the essential role played by property structures in the management of resources was recognized in Hardin's famous article on the 'Tragedy of the Commons,'" and that "some authors have proposed the 'privatization' of international commons to make their use by various nations more efficient." Such initiatives, they note, are "at the root of tradable permit schemes largely incorporated into the Kyoto Protocol of the Framework Convention on Climate Change..."[4] These arguments suggest that the theoretical power of the "tragedy" has outstripped a nuanced understanding of the nomadic pastoralist systems it emerged from. While there is an increasing body of literature dedicated to the behavior and importance of non-state actors in such negotiations, nomads are often contained, dismissed, or marginalized within a broad "developing world" category. Though at higher risk from climate change than the developed world,[5] it is assumed "marginal" producers like nomads are less able to deal with the problem. Luterbacher and Sprinz again: "Common to the marginal systems in all historical periods are the absence of redundancies in their production systems that would allow adaptation to sudden changes, and little capital (other than land) that would permit rapid changes of production strategies."[6]

Likewise, mainstream media, even when it is explicitly sympathetic to the relevant nomadic populations, consistently frames nomadism and conservation in terms of a Hardin-centered debate. It lends equal credence to both sides. The *Christian Science Monitor*, for example, reported on the plight of the Van Gujjars, a nomadic population local to the foothills of the Indian Himalayas. "'Buffalo herders,'" the author reported, "'are banned from the park because overgrazing and trampling causes environmental degradation,' says G.S. Rawat, a professor at the Wildlife Institute of India." The opposing opinion was reported less forcefully: "'The actual environmental impact of Van Gujjar herds has never been determined,' says Nabi Jha, a scientist studying alpine grasslands in Uttarakhand."[7]

This kind of framing remains the norm despite more than forty years of fierce critical reaction to Hardin's argument, and indeed the terms of the debate. Typically, the counter-arguments rely on anthropological knowledge to complicate Hardin's assumptions about "the commons" and "the herdsman." Neither is uniform or simple. Instead, across nomadic cultures, access to rangeland is regulated by a variety of social institutions which are not immediately legible from a sedentary perspective. These vary from undocumented "conventional" ownership—as Barfield observed in Afghanistan[8]—to the fluid open-access systems in Kenya that Terrence McCabe focuses on.

McCabe explicitly oriented some of his anthropological work towards debunking Hardin, as did many others. In fact, a raft of comparative quantitative studies illustrate the environmental benefits of nomadic pastoralism *v.* privatization and subsequent ranching, agribusiness, resource extraction and other factors.[9] And yet none of these arguments have proven as tenacious as Hardin's—or indeed, as influential. As McCabe writes,

> ...Hardin's article was published just prior to the onset of the Sahelian drought in which hundreds of thousands of livestock died and an unprecedented destruction of productive rangeland was observed. Donor agencies and national governments adopted the position that pastoral nomadism was inherently destructive to the environment and advocated the implementation of development programs that in one way or another attempted to privatize formerly communal rangelands.[10]

In McCabe and many others' analysis, those projects have met with "almost uniform failure."[11] Furthermore, the increasingly vocal nomadic populations in question "insist that they're a natural part of the environment and help maintain balance within the forests [or other commons] they rely upon for survival. They assert that because they've been returning to the same areas for hundreds of years, their grazing practices must be sustainable."[12] The scientific and anthropological communities largely agree and have coalesced in the anti-Hardin camp—even if they have not debunked "the tragedy" in every instance.[13]

Why, then, does the pro/anti-Hardin framing remain so widely accepted? One explanation is that his argument constitutes a fundamental structural relationship, whereas the counter arguments tend to be case specific. The "tragedy" is readily generalizable. Hardin's work has been integrated into an extraordinary array of disciplines, from economics to evolutionary psychology. There is no doubt it has been a persuasive theory.

With slight revision, it is ultimately so strong that—contrary to decades of interpretation—it can itself account for sustainable pastoral nomadism. Hardin made the necessary revision himself, twenty-five years after the essay's publication:

> To judge from the critical literature, the weightiest mistake in my synthesizing paper was the omission of the modifying adjective "unmanaged." In correcting this omission, one can generalize the practical conclusion in this way: "A 'managed commons' describes either socialism or the privatism of free enterprise. Either one may work; either one may fail: 'The devil is in the details.' But with an unmanaged commons, you can forget about the devil: As overuse

of resources reduces carrying capacity, ruin is inevitable." With this modification firmly in place, "The Tragedy of the Commons" is well tailored for further interdisciplinary syntheses.[14]

Reading this in light of the wealth of information on nomadic resource management systems, it is possible to dissociate Hardin's "tragedy" and nomadism. The "tragedy," as revised, poses no threat to pastoral nomadism because the literature has shown that what was once thought "unmanaged" *terra nullius* is neither, from the Mongolian steppe to the Tanzanian Masai Mara. The problem for nomads, rather, is the failure of the latest scientific and anthropological understandings to achieve wide acceptance and supplant misinterpretation of the "tragedy" and overgrazing. Just as the international political debate over climate change lagged behind scientific certainty in the phenomenon,[15] the discourse around pastoral nomadism lags behind the evidence for its environmental sustainability.

In both cases, the reasons why are numerous and complex. A key factor, as we shall continue to see, is that nomadism poses a threat to states. They are thus reluctant to embrace it, despite its benefits. In this way the practice is comparable to radical emissions cuts, for example, or any other initiative that is good for the environment but potentially costly for a state. There is a calculus. Moreover, debates about nomads and the environment often mask debates about whether nomads have a place in modern states at all. McCabe intuited this when he wrote that: "['the tragedy of the commons'] provided those with an anti-nomadic perspective the theoretical underpinning for their convictions."[16]

The Environmental Consequences of States' Nomadic Policies

The anthropologist Aparna Rao deals incisively with the consequences of those convictions. Within the climate change–conservation discourse, she focuses on the relationship between the creation and management of a national park and pastoral nomads in Kashmir. "Using the example of the Dachigam National Park," she illustrates

> how wildlife management problems are often embedded in the much larger context of state-nomad relations and, more generally, in relations of dominance handed down from colonial times, and closely related to colonial concepts of nature. Finally, I show how such relations of dominance can be contested in times of more generalised political conflict.[17]

Rao's findings, though, reveal more than an extension of colonial structures of dominance. They also illuminate how state policies towards nomads contribute to the environmental problems they are meant to alleviate. It must be noted at the outset that state behavior is not consistent. In the Indian case since the 1970s, according to Rao, some departments have had "excellent special programmes for nomadic pastoralists." But these were the exception. More often, the "Forest Department battled these very herds and their owners" to the detriment of the environment. Patterns in that process of "battle," like designation of national parks in nomadic routes, recur across eco-systems and states.

They begin with state and scientific information collection poorly suited to nomadism. In Kashmir, "not only did these local government departments work at loggerheads, but their data concerning pastoral nomads were entirely contradictory."[18] In China in the same period, "nationwide statistics on rangeland degradation derive from undocumented surveys ... using criteria originally envisioned for the allocation of pasture land following de-collectivization." According to Harris, Chinese degradation and livestock statistics "cannot necessarily be assumed to be accurate or even representative" because they "have a history of being manipulated at both local...and higher government levels."[19] As in Hesse and MacGregor's Kenya case study,[20] the state ultimately favors sedentarist-centric metrics.

Hesse and MacGregor identified the relevant economic consequences, and Rao does too. But she also identifies the environmental consequences: "herds had not increased since 1914, and yet there had been a dramatic increase in overgrazing due to the conjunction of a variety of ill-conceived, and even contradictory, government policies." These policies were sometimes executed in isolation, ostensibly for the prevention of overgrazing, but often they were concurrent with the establishment of a natural park for the sake of wildlife conservation. Grazing taxes, fencing, checkpoint and identification requirements, and roads "cutting across traditional nomadic migration routes...'to avoid nomadic movement...for the convenience of the traffic....'"[21] were all articulated as steps towards environmental protection but often had damaging results. The road construction, for example "led to further erosion, which rose drastically between 1965 and 1980, and drove migrating herds deeper into the forests," and thus contributed to overgrazing.

China's overlapping environmental and nomadic policies result in similar unintended environmental effects. According to US cables, "environmental recovery and preservation are often identified as a priority by provincial and local officials, and are a primary rationale for land contracting and nomad settlement policies."[22] This rationale is in turn justified by "Chinese scientific studies since the 1980s [which] have often cited overgrazing and grassland rodents (voles) as the main causes of desertification." The reality of these rationales and policies, according to a nomadic source on the Tibetan plateau, is that

> ...it is the government's land division and fencing policies that should be blamed for degradation, as they force herds to graze repeatedly in the same area. Traditional rotational herding practices, on the other hand, provide greater flexibility to adjust to conditions and allow grassland recovery as needed...[23]

That nomad source is not a scientist. And as mentioned above, despite the Anglophone anthropological community's skepticism of the "tragedy of the commons," the causes of degradation and consequences of settlement and land enclosure are not universally proven. The Chinese scientific community's arguments undermining nomadic pastoralism remain consistent, even as Anglophone scientists "identify either previous or more recent state policies as the cause of degradation." And according to Harris' comprehensive literature review of the QTP: "empirical evidence showing that sedentarization policies have exacerbated rangeland degradation...is scant. Monitoring rangeland trends in a way that could provide feedback on the biological effects of sedentarization programs has simply been insufficient (or too poorly documented and published) to allow a clear picture."[24]

But the lack of evidence for sedentarization's environmentally damaging effects does not undermine positive arguments for sustainable nomadism. Harris concludes with an anti-Hardin, anti-Chinese state argument:

> As with any cultural-economic system, [nomadic pastoralism] may be sustainable under certain external circumstances and not under others. But it does appear logical that the mere fact that most rangelands of concern are considered to have been in much better condition only a few decades ago is sufficient to conclude that traditional pastoral systems can be consistent with long-term sustainability, and thus cannot, of themselves, be identified as a cause of degradation.[25]

Lacking certainty, this is the convincing Anglophone-consensus argument on the environmental effects of pastoral nomadism. Politically, it has serious implications—not least that in order to be environmentally responsible, states must sometimes make space for pastoralist nomads.

Nomadic-Environmental Policy as a Technique of State Control

It is often unclear whether states' rejection of that consensus argument is authentically based upon environmental concerns at all. At the least, it is informed by other considerations. As Harris (under) states:

> Because most pastoralists are Tibetan, Mongolian, or other non-Han ethnic minorities whereas political authority rests largely in the hands of Han Chinese and because discussion of ethnic tension remains a sensitive issue in China, dispassionate analysis of rangeland degradation has been constrained by its close association with politically charged issues.[26]

In this context, it is unsurprising that China's environmental policies are repeatedly bound up in efforts to sedentarize nomads who have traditionally lived beyond government control. The PRC's scientific community's findings explicitly buttress those efforts. For example, several recent Chinese studies "list 'traditional' or 'backward' practices on the part of pastoralists as a cause of degradation, without specifying which practices they mean."[27] Following from this pejorative generalization, Chinese research "has generally paid little attention to the ecological, economic or social sustainability of [alternative] proposed livestock management systems."[28] The lack of attention to ecological consequences— the stated problem—suggests that the overgrazing issue is highly instrumentalized by the state for some other purpose.

US cables indicate the same thing. On the Tibetan Plateau, though Chinese justifications have remained environmental, a US analyst notes that "a sense of official urgency to extend government authority over scattered and hard to control nomad communities, stemming from the events of March 2008, appears to be driving the settlement efforts." The events in question—a series of anti-China protests and riots which spilled from Tibet into neighboring provinces[29]—were in turn connected to Tibetan frustration with the "the provincial government's campaign to effectively end nomadic life in the province by 2012." Governments and NGOs estimate that such policies—justified on unrevised "tragedy of the commons" grounds—will "affect a radical restructuring of the lives" of some two million Tibetan nomads.[30] The authors of the US cable saw "little evidence of implementation" of environmentally successful policies. They did see, however, "another potent indicator of the extent to which the government regards these communities as a threat…a large, newly-built People's Armed Police (PAP) base we stumbled across on the outskirts of the county seat."[31]

Environmental policies are not only a mask for sedentarization, security action, and control. They serve major economic purposes for states. The most transparent example is the substantial revenue generated by national parks. Serengeti National Park, which required Masai relocation, is estimated to have generated between $1.4 and 1.9 billion for the Tanzanian government between 2007 and 2017.[32] Less obvious are ways in which resettlement projects themselves can be economic stimulators. The Chinese project on the Tibetan plateau has driven "multiple new housing developments for nomad settlement; upgraded county roads... expanding mushroom cultivation facilities; and preparations for a planned new airport." US analysts note that this development has not been particularly beneficial to the nomads. "Little or none of these developments have resulted in significant new job opportunities for the local population; instead, resulting jobs are mostly going to migrant Han laborers."[33] Like the labor, contracts for these resettlement projects are being awarded to out of region interests allied with central elites: "It is highly likely that most—or even all—of the contracts for these building projects are going to Zigong-based developers, who are also bringing in their own workers."[34]

The Value of "Community Conservation" for Nomads and States

Not every environmental policy involving nomads is so exploitative or blunt. Worldwide, "community conservation" is becoming increasingly popular. But conservation is contingent upon particular conceptions of nature. As Eleanor Fisher writes, "the links between populations' re-settlement and the gazettement of protected areas for conservation are complex and have led people to re-interpret and contest both re-settlement and conservation goals in many different ways."[35] Discussing the Kashmiri park, Rao emphasizes the continuity of elite colonial conceptions: "Dachigam is an exclusive stop for state guests to visit, hunt and stay in, just as it was one hundred years ago—a site for relaxation and sport for the elite." The same is true in formerly British East Africa, where, Martin Enghoff argues in *Nomadic Peoples Journal*, "wildlife conservation, as a form of land use organized by the state...must be considered one of the major forms of alternative use of semiarid pastoral land. Huge tracts have been set-aside as wildlife reserves or national parks, where only tourists can come."[36] There is real conservation in these parks. They are not only tourist traps, or instruments for the suppression of mobility. It was in Dagicham that the earth's remaining Kashmir stag population grew from 127 in 2008 to 218 in 2011.[37]

That said, alternative, nomadic notions of what is valuable in nature have been articulated repeatedly throughout the anthropological litera-ture—Barth's work on Basseri aesthetics focused on this as early as 1961, as did Thesiger's in 1959. That literature is complicated from a post-colonial view. But it is fair to conclude that the nomadic conceptions it addresses have never been deeply embedded in the state structures responsible for setting conservation policy, or their elite alternatives.

Those alternatives have remained largely static conceptually, but the relevant actors have changed. The parks are no longer intended to "'afford health and excitement to British officers serving in India, and relaxation to the soldier...'"[38] Rather, they are for new elite actors: for-eign tourists, and an international wildlife-conservation lobby. Some of these non-state elites began to apprehend the contradiction over the course of the latter half of the twentieth century. None of these is exis-tentially threatened by nomadism. Indeed, they frequently romanticize the practice. And both groups can apply pressure on the state in terms of potential revenue and reputation costs. Rao notes that when the Indian state eased restrictions on the mobility of the Bakkarwals through Dagicham, it did so in part "to please and obtain funding from the largely international and elitist wildlife and environmental lobby...."

Attendant conservation initiatives, however, often remain structures of state dominance over nomads. In Tanzania for example, "the Ngorogoro Conservation Area [NCA] was established as a joint conservation and human use area in 1959, following the forced removal of Masai pastoral-ists from Serengeti National Park." The NCA "was to be the home of the extirpated Masai population in perpetuity." As in the Dagicham National Park case, this did not simply result in the assimilation of nomads into sedentary culture. Indeed, in the Ngorongoro case, the traditionally nomadic Masai population grew from 10,000 in 1959 to 40,000 by the time of the study in 2009. From a nomadic perspective, the conservation policies of the state were still deeply problematic:

> ...resident Masai and their supporters have claimed for a long time that the conservation policies of the NCA Authority have detrimentally affected their economic well being, have undermined their food security and general welfare and are responsible for a downward spiral of economic deprivation.[39]

These complaints are quantifiable. Kathleen Galvin and others' research attempts to assess their accuracy and thus determine how compatible nomadic pastoralism and current conservation efforts are:

> Land use interacts with ecosystem structure and dynamics through such processes as vegetation and herbivore production, which are in turn driven by climate. Development and conservation policies influence land use, with subsequent impacts on pastoral welfare, livestock production, wildlife conservation efforts, and ecosystem integrity...[40]

Taking into account all those factors, the Galvin analysis compares the NCA and another nearby conservation area with less stringent state restrictions in Loliondo. The results manifest themselves in statistically significant nutritional indicators, like the circumference of Masai men's triceps. "The initial comparisons," writes Galvin, "demonstrate that the Masai of Loliondo are better off than the NCA Masai."[41] The situation does not seem particularly prosperous for either group, but the key implication is that the fewer state restrictions, the better off the nomads are. Galvin concludes: "the situation in northern Tanzania is representative of conservation/development dilemmas throughout the drylands of Africa and Asia, results should test applicability of the... approach to other regions."[42]

Galvin also concludes that "the costs of wildlife conservation are partially borne by the residents of conservation areas. Thus area residents will have to be somehow compensated by conservation programmes." This kind of assertion appears frequently in the nomadic-environmentalist arena—even though debates therein are ostensibly waged in scientific terms. Charged normative recommendations are mostly undifferentiated from the rest of the research. Elsewhere, Galvin insists strictly: "we were not able to confirm that the causes of [Masai] problems were rooted in the policies of the Ngorongoro Conservation Area Authority (NCAA)."[43] The juxtaposition of this "hard" science with her normative assertions creates some tension—i.e., if Galvin is not able to prove that Masai problems are the result of NCAA policy, how can she justify calling for compensation? Such an argument draws on a deeper, qualitative post-colonial well. This is especially important given that her methodology was developed in collaboration not only with "NGOs representing Pastoralists (e.g., African Wildlife foundation and others) and wildlife interests (e.g., World Wildlife Fund)"[44] but "government agencies." In this light, the tension in her research suggests how and why the conservation agenda dominates the international discourse on nomadism—it is on the "inside."

The Nature and Effect of International Nomad NGOs

Conservation can thus be read as a "way in" to discussions of a practice that is threatening to states. An example of this is the Dana Declaration on Mobile Peoples and Conservation, which we drew on for our definition earlier in this book. Other conferences and statements on nomadic pastoralism—i.e. from Nairobi in 2013, and Khartoum in 2015—have likewise raised anti-state politics from the less-threatening position of environmental discourse. But the effects of such conferences and the resulting literature have been very been modest in terms of state-nomad relations. The Dana conference website, which presumably would emphasize the success of the project, highlights outputs including "a brochure, a poster, a report on conference proceedings, and a film." More substantial, perhaps, are the resultant endorsements by UN agencies and civil society groups in a variety of countries, and the emergence of an international umbrella NGO: the World Alliance of Mobile Indigenous Peoples (WAMIP).

Given the conferences and endorsements, such an organization might seem well positioned to advocate on behalf of nomads, especially given a growing understanding (here represented by Urs Luterbacher) that "… the rising empirical importance of nonstate actors within international environmental cooperation has brought about greater theoretical attention to their impact and power vis-à-vis states…"[45] But despite the proliferation of such groups over the last decade, the nomadic agenda has received very little attention. In 2002 *The Guardian* dealt with it all like this, in a "society" section paragraph. "'Mobile Peoples' is nothing to do with telephones. It's the new politically correct phrase for nomads, who are under increasing threat not just from dwindling natural resources, they say, but also from the global conservation industry. The name was chosen recently at a meeting in Jordan."[46] Nearly ten years after that paragraph, *The Guardian* published another story under the headline "Uganda: nomads face an attack on their way of life." The story was timed to the 2011 UN summit on climate change in Durban, and its author, John Vidal, reported: "Africa's estimated 20 million nomadic herders will not be directly represented in the talks, but their fate depends on attempts to reduce carbon emissions." This feature, highly sympathetic to nomads, made no reference to any advocacy group, to Dana, or to WAMIP. In the Durban conference and more generally, the nomadic voice is little heard, and usually only heard in terms of "conservation."

Why should this be? Obviously, the distribution of resources between nomad NGOs and states is vastly unequal, as it is in most NGO-state dynamics. But the nature of nomadic advocacy presents particular obstacles. A passage from the World Initiative for Sustainable Pastoralism's (WISP) website is illustrative. In a description of WISP's organizational structure, the website identifies a "Project Management Unit (based at IUCN ESARO), a Pastoral Advisory Group (PAG), a WISP Steering Committee, a global electronic network of over 2000 members (WISPnet) and various partners working on specific knowledge management themes." The PAG, it continues, "is a key mechanism for guiding thematic planning by WISP, setting the agenda for focal areas, and for providing a reality check for the work of the coordination unit." However:

> …regularly meeting with pastoralist representatives worldwide is not a realistic option and the PAG is therefore *an undefined group of pastoralist representatives who are met opportunistically at Global and Regional pastoral gatherings*. In between these meetings WISP tries to maintain the input of pastoralists by working closely with those pastoralist agencies at national and regional levels that have a mandate from pastoralist communities…[47]

The problem for WISP is not only that an "undefined group" has limited continuity and cohesion. More fundamentally, it is that pastoralist focused agencies at the national and regional levels—i.e. the Forest Department of Rao's Kashmir analysis—are often concerned with asserting state control over pastoralist nomads. Kal Raustiala, in his analysis of the growing influence of NGOs on the climate change discussion, argues that much of their success "comes not at the expense of state power, but rather to the mutual advantage of states and NGOs."[48] The threatening nature of nomadism to the state may preclude this mutual benefit,[49] even given nomadic pastoralism's mitigating environmental effects. In this light, it is not surprising that Dana and other nomad-centric NGOs focus on environmental aspects of the practice. According to Dana's website, the Declaration

> …is an attempt to forge a new partnership between conservationists and mobile peoples in order to ensure that future conservation policies and programmes help maintain the earth's ecosystems, species and genetic diversity while respecting the rights of indigenous and traditional communities which have been disregarded in the past.[50]

This definition of nomads Dana articulated for this purpose is in some ways empowering, and others not. "[It] covers indigenous and traditional peoples whose livelihoods depend on extensive common property use of natural resources, and who use mobility as a management strategy and as an element of cultural identity."[51] Attention to common property and mobility as cultural identity speaks directly to state restrictions on nomadism, but the anchoring in the environmental/conservationist discourse does not always represent what is most salient to nomadism—even if it might make space for it in state-centric international discussion.

This does not mean that nomads have yet to benefit from the increase of NGOs like Dana and concurrent emerging norms. Causality is difficult to trace but not impossible to conceive. One cable from the US Consulate in Chengdu recounts an analyst's visit to a nomadic family in the company of Chinese officials:

> During the course of the visit, officials repeatedly emphasized that resettled nomads built their own homes using government subsidies to cover eighty percent of the cost of the dwellings. When asked if he was satisfied with his new home and lifestyle in the presence of local officials, the former nomad replied that he was "very happy." (Note: In a conversation out of earshot of the officials, Congenoff learned that the houses in the village were all built by construction workers from inland China, rather than by the nomads themselves. End Note).[52]

While quick to defend the way in which the nomads are being settled, and how well they are faring once they are settled, they never address the problem of whether they should have been settled in the first place. The Chinese officials, in interactions with the American foreign service, seem aware that they are in danger of transgressing some international norm in their policy of resettlement—just not one specific to nomads. But we can easily imagine the norm evolving in that direction.

Nomadic Resistance in the Climate Change Debate

Nomads resist environmentally justified sedentarization in a variety of ways beyond NGO initiatives. The most obvious is through their familiarity with their environment. This is often overstated. As the nomad analyst ag Youssef noted: "most Touaregs do not 'know the desert': they know the areas which contain their traditional pastures."[53] Still, nomads develop a familiarity with large areas, remote from state control. It is the first defense. In Govind Pashu Vihar National Park, for example, when the state "intimidat[ed] the estimated population of 50,000–70,000 [van

Gujjars] to settle in villages, essentially becoming conservation refugees,"[54] some of them they simply walked around the park and made
camp 4,000 feet higher.

Nomadic communities do not move or resist monolithically, however.
For nomads in Kashmir, Indian environmental policy not only leads to
increased state evasion but increased disparity in the wealth. This is not
simply because, as Rao notes, "certain decisions taken for 'environmental
reasons' by the local state forest, soil conservation and wildlife departments have led to loss of access to traditional pastures." It is also because
of the way in which nomads processed those decisions. Given their
spread over remote areas, nomads as a group become aware of government initiatives more slowly than their sedentary counterparts. Thus,
earlier informed individuals, usually "more prominent community members...[are] able to make alternative arrangements in time; the less well
informed majority is driven to look hastily for short-term solutions that
have often aggravated their difficulties and led to further overgrazing."[55]
This contrasts with sedentary populations, which learn of initiatives
more simultaneously.

Some nomadic representatives, of course, have extremely sophisticated
communications networks, and use them to take advantage of state-centric
NGOs for their own purposes. It is worth examining one nomadic dissident in particular to see how this works, and what resistance looks like
more generally when the option of simply moving away is limited.

In 2007, the Mongolian Tsetsegee Munkhbayar received The Goldman
Environmental Prize. According to the BBC, it "is sometimes known as the
Nobel prize for the environment."[56] The prize "recognizes individuals for
sustained and significant efforts to protect and enhance the natural environment, often at great personal risk," and is administered by the The
Richard and Rhoda Goldman Fund. According to its website, the fund is
characterized foremost by "a strong connection to the San Francisco community and California, a lifelong concern for the environment, and a deep
and unwavering commitment to the Jewish people and Israel."[57]

Munkhbayar came from a culture far removed. In the press and award
citation, he is repeatedly characterized as "a poor livestock herder" who,
on the basis of his unusual persistence, was elected to his local citizens'
council. According to the Goldman Foundation, this was "a rare occurrence for a non-elite Mongolian herdsman." Thereafter, it continues,
Munkhbayar...

...became increasingly concerned about the shrinking Onggi River and, with the support of the local people, successfully helped to stop destructive mining operations....[He] eventually convinced the government to increase and enforce mining regulations in the region and to stop damaging mining activities and begin environmental restoration.[58]

That Munkhbayar "convinced the government" of anything is a radical oversimplification, if not outright fallacy. It is accurate that the greatest tangible victory in Munkhbayar's career has been the renewed flow of the Onggi River in Central Mongolia, which had stopped as the result of the diversion of river water into high-pressure hydraulic mineral extraction systems.[59] Nomads who camp on the banks of the Onggi River described Munkhbayar's accomplishments in awed tones. According to one, what he did was "a miracle." "Munkhbayar turned the water back on," he said, "he is like a god here."[60]

Others familiar with Munkhbayar often stated that his arguments spoke directly to their problems. His emergence as a leader was extremely valuable not only because of government attitudes, but because of the nature of the local nomadic community. Nomads repeatedly explained that "herder associations...are all meaningless things."[61] Why this should be is a puzzle, but mobility, an individualist suspicion of authority, and state intransigence were all consistently provided as explanations. As one woman put it: "We do not have leaders among our families. We are talking at the same level."[62] The emergence of a single charismatic leader was thus unusual and valuable.

However, opinion about Munkhbayar across the country is divided, and suggests the complexities of nomadic resistance in the context of environmental advocacy and conservation narratives. It must be noted, first, that though Munkhbayar is by far the best known advocate of nomads in the country, approximately half of the nomadic households interviewed for this book had never heard of him. Furthermore, some had unclear perceptions of what, exactly, Munkhbayar was well known for. As one herder put it, "he is very famous...he worked as veterinarian. Also as a mechanic."[63]

Munkhbayar's assertion that "all the herders in the countryside think the same as me," is problematic for more reasons than that. Certainly his opinion that government corruption is rampant is widely held, and corroborated by interviews[64] and corruption perception indexes like Transparency International, which consistently place Mongolia in the bottom third of its scale.[65] His fundamental arguments about nomadism, conservation, and the future of the Mongolian state, however, are more radical:

> I think the country would be better off with all of the foreign countries out of the country. Instead, if Mongolia maintains its nomadic traditions it will contribute to the world by being the last spot of healthy living and environment… we want to make Mongolia stay as Mongolia. Make the world stay as the world. I want to make a world where money is not the dominant power.[66]

Munkhbayar is not going to get what he wants, but neither is he a lone radical. His anti-currency attitude, for example, resonates with arguments Agrawal makes about the constructed, hierarchical relationship between commodification, bartering, and currency in India.[67] It also characterizes nomadic herders elsewhere in Asia—in Qiang Prefecture China, for example, where herders "live in a largely cash-free economy."[68]

More significantly, his arguments about the maintenance of tradition speak to what is perhaps the central tension for pastoral nomads in a period of accelerating climate change (and climate change awareness). On one hand, a nomad who happened to be the "nature inspector" for his Gobi *sum* put it like this: "If the weather is good we have totally wonderful life. There is no other freedom such as being a nomad."[69] On the other, within a day's drive of that nature inspector's camp, a woman was anxiously trying to give up nomadic life. "Herders have a hard time of it," she explained.

> …I do not think they even want to be nomads. They do not want to have to stand in snowy, stormy days looking for sheeps. These days are over for them. Only a few people think: as long as I do not have to buy meat it is good to be a nomad.…If you spend ten years in an office then you have many skills. If you spend ten years as a nomad, you just fight the wind.[70]

That interviewee, Jamyansaren, was familiar with Munkhbayar, and slightly skeptical of him. But her skepticism stemmed less from the man himself than from nomadism's reliance on the environment in a time of widespread environmental degradation. Frequently, nomads are not certain if nomadism is best practice for their families.

This doubt is not well represented in international conservation narratives, which emphasize momentum over reflection. The Goldman narrative continues with Munkhbayar's ascent to a position of national and even international influence ("Herder to Statesman"),[71] partly as a result of recognition like the Prize itself. From this vantage, empowered by his non-elite constituency, Munkhbayar was supposedly able to ensure the protection of the environment. He was credited with much reform, including:

> ...the Law on Minerals, which will regulate mining and protect precious waterways. In addition, 35 of the 37 mining operations working in the Onggi River Basin have ceased destructive operations. Erel Mining Company (the most egregious violator) has been shut down and the Onggi River is flowing higher and farther than it has at any other time in the last two years.[72]

Goldman has the facts right, but Jamyansaren is also right to be skeptical. Munkhbayar, who sometimes wears a silver pen clipped in one of his high boots, is simultaneously less of an "outsider" and more of a radical than the literature suggests. His position in Mongolia does not fit into easy narratives about heroic conservationists. He was not only elected to the local council, he was mayor of his *sum*. And while it is true that the "poor livestock herder" has on occasion had camping gear in his office, he shares that office with a television studio.

At the same time, in the years following the prize, he became increasingly frustrated with the government and international business reactions to his campaign. He changed the name of his organization from the Onggi River Movement to Fire Nation, and acquired small arms. In September of 2010, he and several associates opened fire on mining equipment at Canadian run Boroo Gold Mine "after the mining company refused to cease operations that he said were polluting local streams."[73] In April 2011, he staged horse-mounted protests in Sukhbataar Square in which he and his associates fired arrows into the windows of parliament. These are PR stunts, but they involve live bullets and sharp arrows. As one MP, Sanjaasuren Oyun, told *Bloomberg*, "the gentleman who organized this protest has become something of an extremist." Oyun later qualified her statement, though:

> I'm not sure that's the right word. He fired guns near mining equipment last year and now says he and his followers may have to take up arms against the government.... He is a resource nationalist. But here in Mongolia we need to strike a balance. How to be sensible but also populist—yes, we face this tension.[74]

The term "resource nationalist" and the sensible approach Oyun advocates take for granted the benefits of states' perpetual quest for control and legibility; Munkhbayar does not. Focus on the "sensible" v. "populist" tension ultimately misses the point of his demonstration. The more important tension is whether the copper extracted from the Gobi, for example, justifies the environmental damage that threatens nomadism and bolsters sedentarism. Put conventionally, Oyun wants to mitigate the damage for the sake of a growing Mongolian economy and attendant "modern" benefits, but Munkhbayar wants to expel the developing actors and cling to the "traditional."

Between mitigation and radical rejection, however, there is a wide spectrum of thought and action that can be read consistently, wherever nomads are involved in environmentally consequential decisions. In the middle, as one elderly Gobi nomad puts it, "[Munkhbayar] was saying the right thing. But then he did something wrong. He behaved aggressively."[75] The radicalization of Munkhbayar, his unlikely foreign connections, and the breadth of the spectrum he sits on all confound simple narratives about nomads in the international discourse on climate change.

The Value of Nomadic Resistance

The relationship between states, nomads, and INGOs is lopsided. "It is indisputable," as Rao writes, "that the forests of Kashmir and its wildlife are threatened. But the nomads are not the sole culprits; they are simply the most politically expedient culprits."[76] In any contestation of wills, nomads seem always to lose out to states. NGOs can seem powerless in the face of state relocation projects or massive infrastructure development. It can even be argued that they do harm, raising expectations to unrealistic levels. As another Gobi nomad said of NGO representatives and social scientists who had visited her along the chewed up coal plains of the Chinese-Mongolian Border:

> ....we are telling so many people about this. These anthropologists promised they would do so much good. Because we are so close to the road, many people stop by, many people ask questions. There are many petrol stations now and the lands are divided. We want to ask for compensation but we don't know who to address this question to. Our herding life will be finished with the two of us. Because even if our children are nomads, where will they go?[77]

It is difficult to see much NGO success or state flexibility in such data. But there are cases in which INGOs have helped to facilitate improvements. WAMIP, slowly, is increasing its influence, if only by virtue of its personnel placement: the current president, Francis Chachu Ganya, is a

Kenyan MP; the secretary general, Lalji Desai, runs his own nomad-centric NGO in India. And Chatty, despite her occasional frustration with Dana, remains optimistic. She tells a story about some Omani Bedouin who attended one of the Dana/WAMIP capacity-building workshops.

> One of these guys came to New York and reported back to the community.... [afterwards] back in Oman pastoralists blocked the roads leading to the oil refineries until the company would hire locals. They demanded training for 20 young men every year. And they got this out of Oxy [Occidental Petroleum Company]. I've been trying to do this for 30 years! But they always managed to shelve my report...[78]

Chatty acknowledges the number of variables that could have contributed to this political awakening and action. The capacity-building was, no doubt, one of many. And furthermore, she says, "you do what you can, but you can't predict what people are going to do with it." Nevertheless, she helped organize a follow up conference: "Dana + 10." Munkhbayar, likewise, persists in his pro-nomad agenda, despite a recent spell in prison. "There is a Mongolian proverb," he likes to say: "if you have enough courage you will have enough wisdom. The future of the movement? Probably we will have to use both methods, violent and non-violent, depending on the circumstance."[79] Whatever their limited primary impact on states, such actors are clearly having a secondary effect: until roughly twenty years ago, there was no international nomadic NGO network/advocacy movement. Today there is, however flawed or limited.

6

SUMMATION AND THE AGENTIC QUESTION

"For a mighty nation like us to be carrying on a war with a few straggling nomads is a spectacle most humiliating, an injustice unparalleled, a national crime most revolting, that must, sooner or later, bring down upon us or our posterity the judgment of Heaven."

John "Black Whiskers" Sanborn
US Commissioner on Indian Affairs,1867

Myths of nomadism persist. The nomad is cousin to the American cowboy and the Somali *shifta*; he is the acrobat at the edge of the campfire; he roars in the horde that sacked Baghdad; he lives his whole life on a boat in the South China Sea. And so on. Myth is not inherently bad, of course, or out of place in the social sciences. It obviously has political uses—as, for example, in Tsetsegee Munkhbayar's campaign against MNCs in Mongolia.[1] But myth largely is born of ignorance. And ignorance is what most characterizes sedentary attitudes towards nomadism. This is dangerous, and the consequences can be stunning in their violence. In 2012, these myths—and everything else that we have covered so far—converged in Mali with terrible repercussions for one of this book's sources.

On March 21, 2012, a sergeant in the Forces Armées et de Sécurité du Mali, Amadou Sanogo, led a mutiny culminating in the capture of the presidential palace and state television station. He then declared himself President of the National Committee for the Restoration of Democracy

111

and State (CNRDR) and said the borders were closed until further notice. His key grievance was President Amadou Toumani Toure's mishandling of the Tuareg rebellion in the North of the country—he'd dealt poorly with the nomads. That rebellion has multiple historical precedents but was galvanized this time by the return of heavily armed nomads from recent conflict in Libya.[2] Their relationships with the Malian, Libyan, Chadian, Algerian, Nigerian, and Sudanese states—and various pan-African and Islamic ideologies—are complex, as demonstrated in previous chapters. They had always influenced security, trade, and mangament of the environment, but in the early spring of 2012, this became undeniable when a significant number determined that it was in their interest, remaining perpetual mobile, to return to Mali to join the country's most prominent rebel group, the MNLA. In the chaos following Sanogo's coup, the MNLA captured much of northern Mali, including the city of Timbuktu. On April 6, 2012, it declared the independent state of Azawad.

The state was riven. As Ibrahim ag Youssef—whom we have quoted several times—wrote in a series of emails:

> Mali is in an appalling mess because the state has done very little to build a nation, because our polity think only money. ATT, our former president, did everything he could to get it: preparing an airstrip in the desert for an old Boeing full of coke, selling hostages for AQIM, not to mention public money....The mess—very much a consequence of ATT's incompetence and corruption—led to the silly putsch and, also, to the declaration of independence of Azawad by MNLA.

Such problems affect everyone along the nomadic—sedentary spectrum. But the situation in Mali remains particularly difficult because so much of the Saharan population tends to nomadism, and the international community, as we have seen, has great difficulty seeing politics from a nomadic perspective. The MNLA rebellion is defined not just by its secessionist agenda, but also by its mobility and trans-nationality. It threatens the security of the whole region, rather than a single state. Understanding it requires attention to the Saharan nomadic population holistically, rather than Mali—or any other state—alone. Further, it requires an understanding of how nomads have been marginalized, and how nomadism is fundamentally a practice of relation to the state.

As far back as 2007, it was clear in the course of research for this book that ag Youssef himself, quoted above, was dedicated to this understanding. This is part of why the African Union seconded him to Sudan to mediation efforts involving the nomads of Darfur. Youssef liked the work, but knew that it was flawed. Though he had greater insight into nomadic problems[3] than some other international analysts working in Darfur, he was unable to speak Arabic, and therefore hobbled. He was alert to this problem. But there was such a dearth of experts on the politics of nomadism—let alone actual nomad analysts—that he was a valuable asset despite his language handicap. It was a good hire by the African Union.[4] International thinking about the nomadic situation in Youssef's Mali, however, has not been so good. The core of his analysis of it is this:

> It is obvious that regional and international organizations should know their members better, pay more attention to the people, beyond the states. They should add some pragmatism to their understandable condemnation of unconstitutional doings.

This sounds platitudinous but, like most platitudes scrutinized, is relevant. It encapsulates much of what troubles the relationship between the states, international organizations, and nomads. The "unconstitutional doings" are the coup and the declaration of a new state. These incidents threaten the international system but are familiar to it. Sanctions were imposed. Individual states, ECOWAS, the UN, and a variety of other institutions rushed to mediate. But, as they did so, they continued to fail to "pay more attention to the people beyond the states." Though the rebellion has its genesis in the marginalization of a population ranging across the western Sahel, the reaction has been focused on Bamako.[5]

Bamako is not purely sedentary any more than the rural Sahara is purely nomadic. In fact, Youssef, like many well to do nomads, kept a house there. He does not any more. In the run up to the coup, he suffered the wrath of an urban population which, like the international community, tends to view the nomadic Tuareg monolithically. He wrote from exile:

> Hard times indeed! I am in Nouakchott, Mauritania. 1st February, my home was one [sic] the first to be attacked, looted and burnt by a mob presented as angry soldiers' wives demanding full information about their men fighting the MNLA...I was in the house with my little stepdaughter, but we somehow escaped unharmed. The whole family, penniless, had to fly out of the country....Hardly any Tuareg left in Bamako and southern Mali these days. 200,000 refugees and internally displaced.[6]

Youssef reflected in later correspondence "the saddest thing in the human tsunami that destroyed our home was the presence of small children in the mob."[7]

It would be incorrect to argue that misapprehensions of nomadism were the sole or even primary cause of what happened to Ibrahim and his family. What is undeniable, however, is that unreflective sedentarization and mediation schemes in Mali foment instability, just as they do in the Hazarajat, and outside of Kismayo. And that pastoral meat production is misreported both in the Masai Mara and on the Mongolian Steppe; that ecological degradation on the Tibetan Plateau is blamed on nomads, just as it is in Kashmir. To our collective loss, nomads remain "other."

This is an old story. Indeed, in the Anglophone tradition, the most famous nomad is probably Cain—the first criminal. But we would do well to recall here that Cain was a farmer before he was a wanderer. It is not too much to hope that, with persistent work, settled and nomadic might keep each other as brothers, no matter Cain's famous question.

A Way Forward?

But how? Ideally, there is much that emerges from this book to benefit students of international politics. While it eschews globalization, security studies, or "the state" as its unifying prism, it has sought to distill sources and arguments that might aid those working in each of these and other international relations sub-fields. In the first instance, nomadic aversion to borders, interaction with NGOs and MNCs, and transnational trade networks contribute to an understanding of the manifestation and effects of globalization. Likewise for security studies, an international relations focus on nomadism can be read as a broadening of the discipline, with implications for topics such as the responsibility to protect, or food security—as we saw in chapter three around the UN "Janjaweed" Resolution, and chapter five, around the "Tragedy of the Commons." And for any scholar who does not regard the state as a black box—that is, almost all outside of the Realists[8]—it provides insight into the sociology of the state: what makes a state legitimate; what kind of pressure comes from "below;" what constitutes state identity. More broadly, in terms of the critical tradition of international relations, the book draws on and develops ideas of interdisciplinarity and anti-state-centrism, which are themselves hallmarks of that tradition. Indeed, reliance on a single discipline, source material, or unit of analysis—particularly the state—would have made the preceding analysis impossible to execute, or even conceive.

This is part of why the book began by asserting that there is no consensus on the definition of nomadism and offered a short history of the field, tracing a heretofore unconnected political/international relations tradition within it. This tradition contributed to the book's own definition of nomadism, namely: the practice of perpetual mobility as political expression essential to cultural identity and livelihood. This definition reflects nomadism's history of relating to but not depending on the state; collapses the political, cultural, and economic; is easily identifiable and tends towards inclusivity. Nor does it exclude the economic, conservationist, or other views that have enriched nomad studies. Rather, it emphasizes nomad-state relations and brings the topic into the field of international relations. Particularly, the theoretical work illustrated nomadism's relevance to sophisticated state-centrism as articulated by Stephen Krasner; mainstream conceptions of property based on the work of John Locke; and the emergent indigenous peoples' rights regime.

The book went on to demonstrate nomadism's relevance to international relations in security, economic, and conservation contexts. It came to conclusions within each field. In terms of global security, chapter three analyzed the effects of nomadism on policy and behavior in five common relations, defined jointly by nomadic and sedentary actors. These relations appeared in combination, especially in instances of what Mary Kaldor characterized as "new war." They conceptualized nomadism respectively as an existential threat to sovereignty; an asset in military campaigns; a strategy of reconciliation; an incubator of terrorism and criminality; or an inseparable element of racial identity.

Chapter four used the relationship between nomadism and the global economy to question dominant economic narratives by presenting five systems which nomadism renders illegible to state and conventional indicators: livestock production; distribution of aid; overland staple and narcotics trading; extractive-industrial investment in educational development; extractive-industrial land acquisition. The chapter provided examples of actors advocating the dominant economic system in each instance and showed how nomads undermined and/or operated around those systems. It concluded by discussing Arun Agrawal's work on nomadic bartering, critically considering conventional ideas about economic progress.

Chapter five critiqued Hardin's "tragedy of the commons" and its dominance in discussions of nomadism and the environment in international relations. and media. It then located and illustrated five nomad-state relationships which drive behavior around conservation. These were: policies on nomads which contribute to the environmental problems they are meant to alleviate; instrumentalization of Hardinesque arguments for security and economic purposes; joint nomad-state "community conservation" projects; international NGO advocacy for nomads; and nomadic resistance.

The topic could be developed beyond these sections in a variety of directions. All would ideally involve more collaboration with nomads. Certain academic methodologies engage and enlarge the population of scholar nomads: systematized oral history; immersive anthropological field work; the invitation of nomads to academic institutions; the support of research and writing they might undertake (such publications could usefully be added to Rio Tinto's leaflets on FPIC in the Gobi); all these, whichever region or nomad related topic they focused on, would enrich our understanding.

To make its larger points about the political nature and relevance of nomadism in the current international system, this work has alighted on a wide range of complicated situations, and many of these are worthy of further investigation. The history of the World Alliance of Mobile Indigenous Peoples (WAMIP) should begin to be recorded while the organization is young; research on the economic benefits of nomadic state evasion (along the lines of Peter Little's work in Somalia, or Hesse and MacGregor's in Kenya) is needed in China and Afghanistan; Cynthia Chou's extensive work on the Orang Laut in Indonesia has provided a brilliant base for investigation into the political history of nomads in that region, where focus on sea based state-evasion could prove as valuable as Scheele's reorientation of scholarship on West Africa towards the Sahara, or Scott's analogous work on the upland massif of Southeast Asia. More extensive archival work in any of the states in those regions could offer increased insight into the nature and history of nomadism in the international system.

Such historical investigations would support research on an array of contentious contemporary international relations problems around nomadism, i.e.: the Libyan recruitment of nomads and their continuing role in the Arab Spring, and in the Syrian civil war; the relationship between nomadic populations and radical religious groups; the legal efforts of the Canadian First Peoples, the Australian Aboriginals, and certain Native American groups; the potential privatization of the Mongolian steppe; the independence movement of the people of Southern (what most call Inner) Mongolia; and the relationship between certain Bedouin and the Israeli military, to name only a few potential lines of inquiry.

Those issues fall under a rubric of security, economics, and conservation drawn directly from this work. There is also room for further study of the arts. Bedouin novels are being published with growing frequency[9] and the Tuareg influenced music of Francophone West Africa is coming to increasing international prominence.[10] These examples suggest the fruits of critical-artistic engagement with nomadic populations around the world. Put another way, the Bedouin are unlikely to be the only nomads writing novels—but these are the only nomadic novels currently in the gaze of the Anglophone academy.

This study has also raised more general questions within that academy. The problem most apparent in connecting nomadism with international relations is the widespread view that what is happening below the state level is not of critical importance to the field. As a discipline, international relations reifies cultures—often, if unintentionally—in the maintenance of state centrism. Chapter one engaged this problem explicitly through a discussion of territoriality, international law, and property, but problematizing the dominant understanding of these ideas is an ongoing critical project. In this light, nomads are one of many potential communities underrepresented in the field of international relations.

Policy Implications

One of the things this book has not done so far is proscribe policy. In doing so, it is necessary to ask at what level of policy-making such recommendations might be executed. At their most ambitious, the following are aimed at state decision-makers and could alter a foreign or interior ministry's conception of and reaction to nomadism. The recommendations are also relevant for "lower level" actors like state security apparatuses (e.g. the American armed forces), NGOs, or diplomats who execute but do not articulate state policies. It is important to note at the outset of any such prescriptions that while the categorical analysis this work engages in helps to provide an intellectual frame, the most pressing nomadic problems are best dealt with on a case by case basis. Indeed, it was the high modernist, categorizing projects of sedentarization, urbanization, and modernization which, in ignoring the detail of the nomadic populations they sought to incorporate, did such harm to them.

With that in mind, there are some clear policy implications for the book's arguments. Education is a key field for the future of nomad studies. Mobile schools and clinics already exist.[11] The effectiveness of these operations and potential problems need further exploration so that they become credible, multiply, and flourish. It is education, on the sedentary and nomadic sides both, which will do the most to combat the fundamental misapprehension that nomadism and modernization are mutually exclusive. The question of what would be taught in such a mobile educational system must be worked out, but a foundational idea would have to be that sedentarization should be consultative, optional process involving the people in question.

That, of course, is a recommendation independent of its place on any curriculum. The challenges are stark in terms of identifying representative members of the nomadic groups; communication costs; potential extractive resource profit loss; and even security. But these costs should be borne, and willingly, in the belief that sedentarism is not inherently more valuable than mobility. This has obvious ancillary implications too numerous to list comprehensively. To take a few examples: for the United States, it means that the State Department and military should not uncritically support the settlement of the Kuchi population in Afghanistan and Pakistan. For the Chinese government, this means an end to the repression of dissident herders in Inner Mongolia and on the Tibetan Plateau. For Rio Tinto and the Mongolian state, this means a real dedication to the principles of Free and Prior Informed Consent. For the United Nations, this means officially disaggregating its policy and language on the Janjaweed. And for nomadic groups—such as the National Movement for the Liberation of Azawad (MNLA), or Munkhbayar and his Fire Nation—it means a dedication to dialogue instead of violence.

Recurring Problems

The arguments that brought us to these points are carefully considered, but criticism could be brought against them. For chapter two, a critical line of argument might be that the anthropologists of the latter of half of the twentieth century and today grasped fully enough that nomadism is "political" and that a book along these lines is redundant. Another might be that the political tradition traced in the history of nomad studies is itself over-blown. Not only does the chapter read too much into the work of scholars like Ibn Khaldun and Volney, it chooses those thinkers selectively and without due attention to the other researchers who worked on nomadism. Moreover, a close reading of these thinkers' work, even if historically interesting, has tenuous or no relevance to problems later examined, i.e. Chinese environmental policy, UN Resolution 1556, or Rio Tinto's investment in Mongolia. It is "academic" in the worst, most meaningless sense of the term—that is, the non-academic actors it purports to analyze might not only dismiss the relevance of its form but the substance of its arguments. Members of the United States' foreign service could reject chapter three's analysis of Kuchi-US-Hazara relations on ethical as well as analytical grounds—on the basis of repeated and well documented atrocities. Rio Tinto would reject chapter four's analysis of nomadic economy in the Gobi—on the basis both of disputed facts, and the Dependency Theory arguments about trans-national elites. And the Chinese state would almost certainly reject chapter five's characterization of its environmental policy as instrumentalized to control nomads.

Even more troublingly, nomads themselves might reject elements of this book, or indeed its whole premise. As noted in chapter two, Sneath and Humphrey identify nomads who agree with them that the category is no longer useful. On what basis, such a person might ask, does this book call me a nomad, when I reject the term? This itself could be read as a form of neo-colonial thinking, mired in romanticism and dedicated to Western academic dominance through expertise on the "exotic," or outright insensitive ignorance. Interviews were conducted through translators—part of the argument would run—and real understanding requires fluency in the given language. This argument is corollary to various nomads' understandable surprise at this researcher's insistence, usually over tea, on similarities between peoples a world away from each other.

An awareness of all these criticisms has informed the project, beginning in chapter one, when the book addressed problems inherent in generalization by introducing ideas about social totality and interdisciplinarity. The subsequent issues have also been examined. In terms of political anthropology and close reading, the relevant issue is not what has been done before, but what can be added by working at a more theoretical, international relations slanted level. Questions surrounding disputed facts arise from particular State/MNC (i.e. US/Rio Tinto) narratives which this book examines, via access to a wider range of sources (Wikileaks, interviews) than such actors provide or consider. In each instance, the book has sought comment on such issues from those actors as best it can. Nonetheless, antagonists might argue that the arguments are simply not backed up strongly enough. Rio Tinto might conceivably call the arguments accusations, and point out that they are presented here on the basis of seven years intermittent, mostly un-systematized research, the selective deployment of secondary sources, and the close reading of illegally leaked cables.

From a parallel but more academic perspective, critics could emphasize the difficulty of ascribing action and power to a category of people beyond statist recording agendas—no matter the sources, selection, and transitivity—and suggest the book relies on an overstated agentic view of nomads. To conclude, this criticism is worth considering in some detail. It returns us, usefully and symmetrically, to the theoretical questions with which we began our investigation.

The Agentic Question

The challenge of ascribing action and power to groups largely outside the statist agenda is widely acknowledged. It is a challenge which remains at the heart of the critical tradition which this work emanates from—not only in international relations, but across disciplines, both for nomads and observers of nomadism. One reason for this is that the most public of nomads appear in seemingly impotent positions, e.g. groups like WAMIP, which we considered in the final pages of the previous chapter. Such groups are rare, vocal self-identifying examples of nomadic agency; but, as we have seen, they accomplish little. Or, put another way, they have limited agency in the international system. At a UNEP-sponsored conference for such groups in December 2013, for example, the output was essentially three recommendations: "1. UN international pastoralist/nomads day; 2. UN endorse the declaration on livestock keepers' rights; 3. Migratory routes must be demarcated, mapped, preserved, and given property facility stopovers International/Cross-Border routes inclusive! [sic]"[12]

Especially in the context of international relations—a field born of the desire to prevent war, in which the nature and exercise of power are guiding lights—these recommendations seem not only impotent but incoherent. Modest to the point of irrelevance in the first two instances and impossibly ambitious in the third, none of the three is likely to be executed. The voices of nomadic representatives who operate in such a conventional state-international contexts tend to get stuck in similar conferences, which state power-brokers consider toothless, if they consider them at all. This conference, for example, was held on the outskirts of Nairobi—but none of the Kenyan government officials scheduled to participate attended. Even the lead organizer for the UN was absent much of the time. Accomodation provided was poor—indicative that little respect was afforded the event. Halfway through the week, a thunderstorm flooded the nomadic representatives out of their tents, forcing them to remove to a polytechnic institute. They complained, as they had throughout the conference, of lack of wifi. The conference, then, did not seem at all a locus of agency in the international system.

But it is a function of state systems' antipathy to nomadism, which we have explored, that this form of nomadic agency—which is most legible to states—is weakest. If nomadism were only manifest at conferences, the case for nomadic agency in an international system of armies and stock markets would be weak indeed. It is not. The bulk of this book has been concerned with nomadism's hidden but stronger expressions: manipulation of the securitization of mobility, maintenance of trade illegible to states, distribution of resource commons. These constitute the essence of the practice, and justify an agentic view on mainstream international relations's traditional terms, in which agency is typically demonstrated by bodies, dollars, and climate change indicators.

In conclusion, however, some further theoretical work on the assumptions upon which interrogations of nomadic agency are based is appropriate. Crucially: is it really "difficult to ascribe action and power to groups outside the state agenda," as this section began? Might, instead, the assumption of inherent challenges to the nomadic agency itself orient us towards the conventional agenda—rather than towards political understandings more sympathetic to an agentic view of nomads?

From a political philosophical perspective, the idea of agency—whether at the personal or group level—remains fruitfully open for debate. Two traditions of thought compete. Analytic philosophers, like Philip Pettit,[13] Michael Bratman,[14] and David Velleman,[15] to take three leaders in the fields, tend towards an individualistic, post-Enlightenment framework. They question whether collective agency is possible at all—and if it is, whether it is something more than the sum of individual intentions/agency. In the spirit of interdisciplinarity with which we began this work, it is important to acknowledge these concerns about agency. But more valuable in the context of nomadism's position in international relations is the comepting view of agency, emerging from those philosophers dealing with Hegel and the tradition of intersubjective identity formation—analogous to "Constructivism" (see Wendt, Ruggie, et al.), in international relations terms. One of the preeminent philosophers of this tradition, highly concerned with agency, is Axel Honneth. In his 1995 work *The Struggle for Recognition: The Moral Grammar of Social Conflicts*, Honneth observed that, until the late twentieth century, political science was "so wedded to the standard model of the collective pursuit of interests that the moral grammar of social struggles had to remain hidden from it." He goes on:

> This only changed…after the methodological intersection of social anthropology and cultural sociology gave rise…to a form of historiography that was able to percieve more broadly and more accurately the normative presuppositions of the way lower social classes engaged in conflict…[16]

In our context, this is distillation and reminder of a large and highly developed body of theory which supports our contention that though nomads do not, as a traditionally illegible category, obviously appear to be pursuing collective interests like states or conventional units, they still have agency in systems of international relations. Honneth traces this reading to E.P. Thompson, Andreas Griessinger, and Barrington Moore, all of whom, though focused on the sedentary, are in the same critical anthropological tradition as Clastres, Scott, Lattimore and this work. With regard to the intersubjective conception of political struggle (in our terms, international relations) that this tradition contributes to, Honneth further notes: "the suggested conception…asserts nothing about the degree to which actors have to be aware of the driving moral motivation of their action."[17]

This is not to say that intention does not matter. It does. Rather, the lack of intention is not grounds for exclusion or omission from a system of political understanding. "The advantage of this approach," Honneth finds, "lies in its heightened attention to the horizon of moral norms of action that are involved in everyday life."[18] The disadvantage: "the events depicted always retain something of the character of mere episodes."

SUMMATION AND THE AGENTIC QUESTION

It is possible to point to this disadvanatage as evidence against an agentic view of a dispersed category like nomads. But to do so is a missed opportunity. It is truer to the research, equally observant of the theoretical tradition, and ultimately more constructive to conceive of the model:

> ...no longer solely as an explanatory framework for the emergence of social struggles, but also as interpretive for a process of moral formation."[19][20]

This is what we have attempted: explanation, grounded in empirical evidence but dedicated to the proposition that such work is inextricable from the ongoing formation of our morals. This book can not definitively answer the agentic question, any more than it can escape the reality that actors involved in the processes it analyzes—from anthropologists like Sneath and Humphreys, to the Kuchi MPs, to American military officers—are equally sophisticated, often better informed, and sometimes more deeply invested in the subject matter. But what it can do, in a spirit of collaboration rather than as the final word on any puzzle, is to argue, to this concluding line, that nomadism is a form of political expression.

ACKNOWLEDGMENTS

Altogether elsewhere, vast
Herds of reindeer move across
Miles and miles of golden moss,
Silently and very fast.

from THE FALL OF ROME
W.H. Auden, 1940

This short book has been a long time coming. I've had a lot of help—
foremost from the nomadic families who welcomed me, fed me, and
answered hours of questions.

Dr. Amia Srinivasan provided some key thinking and reading on
moral philosophy for the last chapter. Likewise Dr. Jeremie Gilbert on
international law, for the first.

Dr. Sudhir Hazareesingh patiently shepherded this project through
continental philosophy and the University's equally dense bureaucracy.

Dr. Dawn Chatty, a preeminent nomad scholar and activist of several
generations, provided sound edits and primary source material.

The book owes a special debt to Dr. Michael Hart. Like decades of
students before me, I benefited from his insightful notes—but more
importantly, from his highly developed sense of irony, his generosity, and
his insistence on finishing what you start. Oxford is lucky to have him.

On the nomad conference circuit, the great journalist Roopa Gogenini
has been a stalwart companion. On various research trips, I have become
particularly indebted to Dr. Ali Safi, Dr. Alex de Waal, Dr. Ibrahim ag
Youssef, Tseren Enebish, Badruun Gaardi, and Anders Oskal.

ACKNOWLEDGMENTS

Thanks to Michael Dwyer and everyone at Hurst & Co. And thanks to the great Dr. Tommy Wide for introducing me to them.

Finally: for getting me into anthropology to begin with, and many years of friendship since, I am most grateful to Dr. Cheryl Makarewicz.

NOTES

"Having no destination I am never lost."

Ikkuyu, c. 1400

1. NOMADISM: ITS RELATION TO THE INTERNATIONAL SYSTEM

1. Rosenberg, *The Empire of Civil Society*, p. 3.
2. In the sense of Robert Cox's distinction between "critical theory" and "problem solving theory."[2] The latter accepts inherited situations, tries to solve problems within them, and tends towards maintenance of the status quo. The former questions prevailing power relationships and inherited situations.
3. Buzan and Richard, *International Systems in World History*, p. 183.
4. Scott, *The Art of Not Being Governed*, pp. 14–16.
5. Via Wikileaks; during the period of research, cablegatesearch.net functioned like Google or other standard search engines.
6. "nomad, n. and adj." OED Online. March 2012. Oxford University Press. Accessed April 24, 2012.
7. Salzman, *Pastoralists*.
8. A close reading of this and other definitions often provides more insight: the second clause of this one, for example does not imagine nomadism as normal—it emphasizes an abnormality: *no* permanent home. But such extended readings are the topic of another paper.
9. Sneath and Humphrey, *The End of Nomadism?*
10. See chapter 6 for a review of the literature.
11. "The settlement of a nomadic people in a permanent homeland or place of habitation." "sedentarization, n." OED Online. March 2012. Oxford University Press. Accessed April 24, 2012.
12. Sneath, p. 1.
13. Rosenberg, p. 4.

14. Tooze, "The Missing Link".

15. E.g.: Huhung and family, author interview, north of Tavan Tolgoi, Mongolia, September 26, 2011.

16. Bussow, "Bedouin Historiography in the Making: An Indigenous History of the Hasana Tribe in Syria."

17. E.g., the Segovia Declaration.

18. Dana Committee, *The Dana Declaration On Mobile Peoples and Conservation.*

19. Chatty, author interview, December 12, 2011.

20. General Conference of the International Labour Organization, *Convention Concerning Indigenous and Tribal Peoples in Independent Countries.*

21. Kingsbury, Benedict, "Indigenous Peoples".

22. Booth, p. 109.

23. "Of, belonging to, or concerned with the form, organization, and administration of a state, and with the regulation of its relations with other states." "political, adj. and n.". OED Online. March 2012. Oxford University Press. Accessed April 24, 2012.

24. See "political expression" in UN General Assembly, *Universal Declaration of Human Rights*, Paris, 1948.

25. Whose character shall be explored throughout following chapters.

26. Chatty, 2011.

27. Glubb, *Handbook of the Nomads, Semi-Nomads, Semi-Sedentary Tribes of Syria.*

28. Chatty, "The Bedouin in Contemporary Syria: The Persistence of Tribal Authority and Control."

29. Glubb, "The Bedouins of Northern Arabia", p. 13, referenced in Elphinstone, "The Future of the Bedouin of Northern Arabia", *International Affairs*, pp. 370–375.

30. Scott, p. xii.

31. Chatty, 2011.

32. De Waal and Flint, *Darfur: A New History of a Long War.*

33. Scott, p. 184.

34. McLaughlin-Chatty email correspondence, "URGENT: Mobile Indigenous Peoples' Concept Paper," June 11, 2004. See especially opening line, and point "1."

35. Thus, while this book does most of its work on pastoralists rather than hunter-gatherers or "service" nomads, it could have engaged the latter populations in the same way—using the work of Hugh Brody in the sub Arctic, for example, or Open Society Foundation reports on the European Roma.

36. Scott, p. 184.

37. Krasner, "State, Power, Anarchism: A Discussion on *The Art of Not Being Governed: An Anarchist History of Upland Southeast Asia*," *Perspectives on Politics*, March, 2011.

38. Buzan, p. 183.

39. Human Rights Watch Report. *Darfur Bleeds: Recent Cross Border Violence in Chad.*
40. Krasner, *Organized Hypocrisy.* See note on Thomson, Deuden, and Cerny, p. 10.
41. Krasner, p. 13.
42. Scott, "Hill and Valley in Southeast Asia...or Why the State is the Enemy of People who Move Around...or...Why Civilizations Can't Climb Hills."
43. Linklater, "Political Community and Human Security", p. 118.
44. Krasner, "State, Power, Anarchism", pp. 79–83.
45. For a succinct definition of this strategy as compared to the more "post-colonial" bent of this paper, see Seth, "Historical Sociology and Postcolonial Theory: Two Strategies for Challenging Eurocentrism.".
46. Locke, *Two Treatises of Government,* Peter Laslett (ed.), 1970. See 2T's chapter "Of Property," 26–36, especially 32, ll. 4–6 *"As much Land* as a Man Tills, Plants, Improves, Cultivates, and can use the Product of, so much is his *Property."* p. 308. Also ll., pp. 28–29 on the topic of "Ore I have digg'd," p. 307.
47. Gilbert, p. 688.
48. Locke, p. 31.
49. See for example: Fisher, Elanore, "Forced Re-settlement, Rural Livelihoods and Wildlife Conservation along the Ugalla River in Tanzania," in Chatty and Colchester (eds), *Conservation and Mobile Indigenous Peoples.*
50. See Gobi author interviews, chapter 5.
51. Quoted in Bautman, "The Sanctuary: the world's oldest temple and the dawn of civilization.".
52. Another legal scholar, Marco Moretti, has self-published his doctoral work in this vein, *International Law and Nomadic People.* Moretti revises an even longer legal history of the relationship between sedentary and nomadic societies. While the work's English is imperfect and its arguments sometimes incoherent, it does contain one especially notable argument, about the sixteenth through nineteenth centuries. "During the period in question... nomadic peoples were considered, in law and in fact, as international actors, holders of sovereignty and international personality, independent from their level of development or their form of political organization." He continues that legal theorists agreed nomads "resided under their own authority by virtue of their first occupation"; and that "the practice of states was consistent with the[se] doctrines." The radical change in attitude towards nomads, he concludes, was a result of the nineteenth century's ascendant legal positivism: "inherent in [this] concept of public international law was the idea of the supremacy of the Western model of culture and system of political organization represented by the state." The idea of Western cultural supremacy, however, was not original to legal positivism. Though Moretti marshals much

evidence, his narrow legal lens diminishes his argument. For example, he considers the sixteenth-century Spanish theologian Francisco Vitoria and his *Lecons sur les Droits des Indians*. This document recognizes that Native Americans in Spanish colonial territory "were the true owners both in public and private law" of their land.[52] This, Moretti argues, is a significant addition to progressive international law. He even calls it a recognition of the Native Americans "right to sovereignty." And it is true that Vitoria, Grotius, and several other authors Moretti discusses recognize the political nature of nomadism, sometimes. Chapter two of this book makes a similar argument, and traces that strain of thought through the history of nomad studies. But Vitoria only argues that the Native Americans were the "true owners," of their land, "before the advent of Spaniards among them."[52] Little good Vitoria's contribution to progressive international law did them after that. None the less, Moretti goes on to argue that the way states dealt with nomads in this period—conquest and treaty-making—"manifested the intention of the Western States to recognize the legal personality and sovereignty of nomadic peoples. In fact," he concludes, "in international law, conquest and treaties are the instruments normally used to transfer sovereign powers, whose transferee is presumed to be in possession." There is a continuing forest-for-trees problem here. Treaties, upheld, might be evidence for recognition of sovereignty. And Krasner, as we shall see, argues that the violation of certain elements of sovereignty in fact reinforce it. But certainly nothing inherent in *conquest* does. Conquest leads to assimilation, even annihilation. In the context of state projects that had been displacing nomads for many centuries before—and during—the nineteenth century, Moretti's argument does not hold up. The elaboration of legal theory with the advent of European legal positivism didn't overturn essentially hostile statist thought towards nomads—it enshrined it.

53. Gilbert, p. 683.
54. Ibid., p. 688.
55. Ibid., p. 714.
56. Though we should be careful not overstate the case. Kingsbury and others have correctly noted that IP rights have proved a mobilizing factor for transnational activity, but the *United Nations Declaration on the Rights of Indigenous Peoples* has extremely limited potential in terms of actual enforcement, and at the theoretical level it essentially sympathetic to states. Article 8, section 2, for example, codifies responsibility for mechanisms of redress and protection of Indigenous Peoples in the hands of the state. This is a fundamental paradox of international human rights oversight (see debates on "R2P" especially).
57. Nicolaidis, Kalypso, author interview, July, 2012.
58. International Committee of the Red Cross. *Protocol Additional to the Geneva*

Conventions of 12 August 1949, and relating to the Protection of Victims of International Armed Conflicts (Protocol I), Geneva, 8 June 1977, Article 1, section 4.
59. Said, "Representing the Colonized: Anthropology's Interlocutors."
60. Krasner, March, 2011.

2. A SHORT HISTORY OF NOMAD STUDIES

1. "Nomad studies," based on the previous chapter's definition, includes any scholarship concerning that political expression which is based on a perpetual mobility essential to identity and livelihood.
2. Khazanov, *Nomads and the Outside World*, p. 1.
3. Irons and Dyson-Hudson, *Perspectives on Nomadism*, p. 2.
4. Dyall-Smith, Mike, "The Autobiography of Weni." Ancient Egypyian Language List. http://www.rostau.org.uk/weniCCER/weni.html
5. Richards, Janet. "Quest for Weni the Elder." *Archaelogy*, Volume 54 Number 3, May/June 2001. http://archive.archaeology.org/0105/abstracts/abydos6.html
6. Breasted, James Henry, *Ancient Records of Egypt*, Chicago: University of Illinois Press, 2001. http://www.reshafim.org.il/ad/egypt/texts/weni.htm
7. Szuchman, Jeffrey (ed.), *Nomads, Tribes, and the State in the Ancient Near East: Cross-disciplinary Perspectives*, Chicago: University of Chicago Press, 2009, pp. 17–20.
8. Breasted, p. 293.
9. The King James Bible. New York: Oxford Edition: 1769; King James Bible Online, 2008.
10. Ibid.
11. Herodotus. *The Histories*, p. 248.
12. Ibid., p. 44.
13. Ibid., p. 235.
14. Ibid., p. 216.
15. Ibid., p. 234.
16. Pervomais'k in Modern Ukraine, *Dictionary of Greek and Roman Geography (1854)* William Smith, LLD, (ed.).
17. Herodotus. *The Histories*, pp. 241–42.
18. Ibid., p. 255.
19. Ibid., p. 231.
20. Chi'en, Ssu-Ma-, *Records of the Grand Historian, Volume 2*. Burton Watson, trans. New York: Columbia University Press, 1961, p. 9.
21. Ibid., p. 164.
22. Ibid., p. 162.
23. Marcellinus, *The Later Roman Empire*, p. 414.
24. Ibid., p. 26.

25. Ibid., p. 424.
26. Pliny the Elder, *Natural History: A Selection*, John Healy. trans., London: Penguin Books, 1991, p. 57.
27. Ibid., p. 414.
28. Arberry, A.J., trans. *The Koran*. New York: Macmillan, 1986, p. 216.
29. Ibid., p. 217.
30. Ibid., p. 123
31. Ibid., p. 226.
32. Ibid., p. 226.
33. Ibid., p. 232.
34. Rosen, "Theorizing from within: Ibn Khaldun and his Political Culture," p. 598.
35. Ibn Khaldun, *The Muqaddimah*, p. 93.
36. Ibid., pp. 118–19.
37. Ibid., pp. 119–20.
38. Ibid., p. 94.
39. Bates, Daniel and Susan Lees, "The Origins of Specialized Nomadic Pastoralism: A Systemic Model," *American Antiquity*, Volume 39, No. 2, April, 1974.
40. Ibn Khaldun, p. 118.
41. Ibid., p. 122.
42. Volney, C.F., *Travels through Egypt and Syria, in the years 1783, 1784 & 1785 Containing the present natural and political state of those countries; their productions, arts, manufactures & commerce; with observations on the manners, customs and government of the Turks & Arabs*. New York: J. Tiebout, for E. Duyckinck & Co. booksellers, 1798, p. 234.
43. Kant, *Political Writings*, p. 230.
44. Brewer, Anthony, "Adam Smith's Stages of History" Discussion Paper, No. 08/601, Department of Economics, University of Bristol, 2008.
45. Hannoum, Abdelmajid, "Translation And The Colonial Imaginary: Ibn Khaldûn Orientalist," *History and Theory*, No. 42, February 2003, p. 61.
46. Ibid., p. 81.
47. Volney, p. 234.
48. Khazanov, p. 10.
49. Irons, p. 3.
50. Ibid., p. 3.
51. Robertson-Smith, W., *Kinship and Marriage in Early Arabia*. Cambridge: Cambridge University Press, 1885.
52. Ibid., p. 36.
53. Ibid., p. 3.
54. They were not the only ones working on the topic though. Dyson-Hudson's

criticism does not make as much sense for Arabic scholars like Abbas al Azzawy or Ahmad Wasfi Zakariya, for example. They were not Malinowskian social anthropologists, but they were at least as intimately acquainted with the Bedouin as the Volney-esque travelers and administrators who had composed ethnographies to that point.

55. Lawrence, *Seven Pillars of Wisdom*, p. 31.

56. Ibid., p. 31.

57. Ibid., p. 223.

58. Brown, Malcolm (ed.), *Secret Despatches from Arabia and Other Writings by T.E. Lawrence*, London: Bellew Publishing, 1991, p. 15.

59. Dyson, p. 5.

60. Evans-Pritchard, E. E., *The Nuer: A description of the modes of livelihood and political institutions of a Nilotic people*, Oxford: Oxford University Press, 1968, p. 15.

61. Ibid., p. 264.

62. Ibid., pp. 264–265.

63. Lattimore, Owen, *Studies in Frontier History: Collected Papers, 1928–1958*. London: Oxford University Press, 1962, p. lv.

64. Lattimore, *Inner Asian Frontiers of China*, p. 71.

65. Ibid., p. 71.

66. Ibid., pp. 77–8.

67. Ibid., pp. 77–8.

68. Ibid., p. xlvi.

69. Ibid., p. 309.

70. Ibid. p. 99.

71. Ibid., pp. 101–2.

72. Pace, "Owen Lattimore, Far East Scholar Accused by McCarthy, dies at 88".

73. Tolstov quoted in Ernest, *State & Society in Soviet Thought*, p. 99.

74. See, e.g., Meir, Avinoam, "Nomads and the state: the spatial dynamics of centrifugal and centripetal forces among the Israeli Negev Bedouin", *Political Geography Quarterly*, Vol. 7, No. 3, July 1988, pp. 251–270; Azarya, Victor, *Nomads and the State in Africa: the political roots of marginality*, Leiden: Rijksuniversiteit te Leiden, Afrika-Studiecentrum, 1996; or Rao and Caisimir, *Nomadism in South Asia*, 2003.

75. Gellner, pp. 99–107.

76. Ibid.

77. Gellner, p. 108.

78. Ibid., p. 105.

79. Khazanov, Nomads and the Outside World, p. 303.

80. Ibid., p. xxxi.

81. Ibid., p. 151.

82. Irons, William, "Nomadism as Political Adaptation: the Case of the Yomut Turkmen," *American Ethnologist*, No. 1, 1974, pp. 635–658.

83. Shakespeare, Nicholas, *Bruce Chatwin*, London: Harvill Press, 1999, p. 14.

84. Ibid., p. 138.

85. Chatwin, Bruce, *Anatomy of Restlessness*, London: Picador, 1997, pp. 100–6.

86. Ibid., p. 140.

87. Chatwin's kind of investigation should be carefully quarantined from works on nomadism which seek positivist credibility, on account of disciplinary divisions in the centers of power where the future of nomadism is up for debate. The professionals in those centers are rightly wary of interlopers—the field attracts dilettantes and romantics. There is a particular type of sari-clad European, often found on the Kenyan coast, who has plans to start a jewelry company named after nomads; motorcycle gangs embroider the word on their jackets; stubbled English majors reference nomads in pursuit of immortality by boxcar. And financiers: "you know I'm such a nomad these days, I fly to New York three times a month, when I'm not headed to Hong Kong." For better or worse, Chatwin could be the patron saint of such people and their inchoate goals.

88. According to a 2007 study, Deleuze is the eleventh most cited author in the humanities, behind Freud, but ahead of Kant. *Times Higher Education*, March 26, 2009. http://www.timeshighereducation.co.uk/story.asp?storyCode=4 05956&sectioncode=26

89. Deleuze, Gilles, and Félix Guattari, *A Thousand Plateaus: Capitalism and Schizophrenia*, trans. Brian Massumi, London: Continuum, 2004, p. ix.

90. Ibid., p. 387.

91. Ibid., p. 4.

92. Ibid., p. 393.

93. Ibid., p. x.

94. This vanguard remains healthy and active, especially, as one reviewer of this work pointed out, in the work of Reza Negarestani and his fictive Iranian archaeologist, Hamid Parsani—see Negarestani's *Cyclonopedia* (2008) especially on the topic of borders.

3. BYWAYS NOT CONTROLLED: THE SECURITIZATION OF PERPETUAL MOBILITY

1. Lederer, Edith M., "UN Council feels heat for peace in Darfur," *The Boston Globe*, June 13, 2006.

2. Reuters Africa, "Russian, Chinese arms used in Darfur abuse—Amnesty," February 9, 2012.

3. Fox News, "Sudanese army attacks South Darfur village," December 11, 2010.

4. *The Scotsman*, "Darfur 'sliding into anarchy,'" November 5, 2005.

5. *The New York Times*, "Times Topics: Omar Hassan Al Bashir," updated July 14, 2011.

6. Crilly, Rob, "'Peacekeeping a struggle in Sudan," *USA Today*, November 30, 2005.

7. Associated Press, "Amnesty: Imported Arms Fueling Darfur Conflict," *ABC News*, February 9, 2012.

8. Lacey, Marc, "Leading Player in Darfur's Drama: The Hapless Camel," *The New York Times*, December 5, 2005.

9. Sather, *The Bajau Laut*, pp. 325–6.

10. Andaya, Leonard, "The Structure of Power in Seventeenth-Century Johor" in Anthony Reid and Lance Castle (eds), *Pre Colonial State Systems in Southeast Asia: The Malay peninsula, Sumatra, Bali-Lombok, South Celebes*, Monographs of the Malaysian Branch of the Royal Asiatic Society, 1974, p. 7.

11. Scott, 2008.

12. Sather, p. 326.

13. Molyneux, J.H., "The Simporna Expedition," *British North Borneo Herald*, 1902, quoted in Sather, p. 49.

14. Sather, pp. 48–59.

15. Ibid., pp. 325–26.

16. Ibid., pp. 45–46.

17. Buzan, Barry, et. al., *Security: A New Framework for Analysis*, London: Lynne Reinner, 1998, p. 24.

18. For more on securitization, Andrew Linklater and Ken Booth in Booth, op. cit., 2005.

19. Op. cit., Buzan, 1998, p. 22.

20. See chapter 1 on Scott, Krasner, and Locke for more on this idea.

21. Sather, p. 49.

22. US Embassy, Kabul. *Local Kuchi-Hazara Deal Dependent on National and International Actors*. June 10, 2009 via Wikileaks. Ref # 211236, "09KABUL 1488".

23. Sather, p. 47.

24. US Embassy, Kabul. *Afghan Human Rights Report On Kuchi-Hazara Violence: Government Inaction Could Lead To More Clashes*. February 3, 2009 via Wikileaks. Ref # 190102, 09KABUL249. Emphasis mine; spelling theirs.

25. Swedish Committee for Afghanistan. "SCA receives big donation for education of Kuchi children." http://www.swedishcommittee.org; Accessed February 21, 2012.

26. Young, John, *Peasant Revolution in Ethiopia: The Tigray People's Liberation Front, 1975–1991*, Cambridge: Cambridge University Press, 1997, p. 150.

27. The same could be said of nomadism decoupled from pastoralism, see point on Scott's similar distinction in chapter 1.

28. Little, p. 16.

29. Korda, *The Life and Legend of Lawrence of Arabia*, pp. 102–6.

30. "Other Government Agency" is a euphemism for the Central Intelligence Agency.

31. US Embassy, Kabul, *Director of Kuchi Directorate: Few Kuchis Will Vote, and Will Vote for Karzai*. August 16, 2009 via Wikileaks. Ref # 090KABUL2382.

32. De Waal, "Counter-Insurgency on the Cheap," pp. 25–27.

33. BBC News,"Q&A: Ethiopia's Afar Region," *BBC News, Africa*, January 18, 2012.

34. US Embassy, Kabul, op. cit., August 2009.

35. See the Manual itself, and Kahl, Colin H. "COIN of the Realm Is There a Future for Counterinsurgency?" *Foreign Affairs*, November/December 2007.

36. Kilcullen, *The Accidental Guerrilla*, p. xiv.

37. IRIN News Network, "Afghanistan: Threat of ethnic clashes over grazing land." UN Office for the Coordination of Humanitarian Affairs, April 7, 2008.

38. US Embassy, Kabul, op. cit., June 2009.

39. IRIN News Network, op. cit.

40. *Hazaristan Times*. "Protests in Italy Against Kuchi Attacks in Hazarajat," June 13, 2010. See especially the picture in which Afghan protestors hold signs referring to Kuchis as "the enemy of civilization." http://hazaristantimes.wordpress.com/

41. IRIN News Network, op. cit.

42. US Embassy, Kabul, "International Human Rights Day: U.S. Embassy Brings Together Civil Society Leaders and Human Rights Activists," Press Release, December 11, 2010.

43. Pashtuns and Kuchis have, it must be noted, sometimes committed terrible crimes in the Hazarajat. See, for example, Human Rights Watch, "Massacres of Hazaras in Afghanistan," New York: HRW, February 2001.

44. US Embassy, Kabul, op. cit., August 2009.

45. US Embassy, Kabul, op. cit., February 2009.

46. Thurston, "Counterterrorism and democracy promotion in the Sahel," p. 50.

47. Quoted in Mundy, Jacob, "Introduction: Securitizing the Sahara," *Concerned African Scholars Bulletin*, 85, Spring 2010, p. 5.

48. Keenan, Jeremy, "Al Qaeda in the Sahel," *Al-Jazeera.com* August 29, 2010.

49. Schmidle, Nicholas, 2009, "The Saharan conundrum," *The New York Times*, February 15, 2009.

50. Al-Qaeda in the Islamic Maghreb/Sahara (AQIM/S).

51. See, for example: Zulaika, J., "The self-fulfilling prophecies of counterterrorism," *Radical History Review*, No. 85, 2003, pp. 191–99; or Mills, "Africa's new strategic significance," pp. 157–169.

52. Mundy, p. 8: "a social scientist whose four decades of on-the-ground experience in the heart of the Sahara, coupled with an impressive publication record, is unrivaled in the Anglophone academy."

53. Keenan, op. cit.
54. For extensive citations, see Mundy.
55. This term is defined (like nomad studies) by the common understanding of agency, modified by this book's new definition of nomadism.
56. Pidd, Helen. "Background: The kidnapping of Edwin Dyer, one of four Europeans seized in West African desert in January reported to have been beheaded by al-Qaida," *The Guardian*, June 3, 2009.
57. Harmon, Stephen,"From GSPC to AQIM: The Evolution of an Algerian Islamist Terrorist Group into an Al-Qaʿida Affiliate," *Concerned African Scholars Bulletin*, No. 85, Spring, 2010.
58. Stratfor Global Intelligence, "The Tuaregs: From African Nomads to Smugglers and Mercenaries," February 2, 2012.
59. US Embassy Bamako. *Observations On Unfolding Hostage Crisis In Northern Mali*. January 29, 2009 via Wikileaks Ref # 09BAMAKO63.
60. Ifeka, Caroline, "War on 'Terror': AFRICOM, the Kleptocratic State and Under-Class Militancy in West Africa-Nigeria," *Concerned African Scholars Bulletin*, No. 85, Spring, 2010.
61. Op. cit., US Embassy, Bamako, January 2009.
62. Isidoros, Konstantina, "Western Sahara and the United States' Geographical Imaginings," *Concerned African Scholars*, Bulletin No. 85, Spring, 2010, pp. 63–64.
63. Ousmane, one of the initial suspects in the kidnapping, denied involvement through intermediaries.
64. US Embassy, Bamako, op. cit., January 2009. Emphasis mine.
65. Isidoros.
66. Ibid., "For example…Iranian Islamic clerics…Lebanon's Shi'ite community.…Al-Qaeda, Pakistan's Taliban, Afghanistan's Taliban, Mali/Niger nomadic Tuareg 'insurgents'.…"
67. Weaver, Matthew, "British hostage Edwin Dyer 'killed by al-Qaida," *The Guardian*, June 3, 2009.
68. Larotourrou, Paul, "Niger nomad speaks out: "We are not terrorists!," *France 24*, October 14, 2010.
69. UN Press Office, "Council Demands Sudan Disarm Militias in Darfur, Adopting Resolution 1556 (2004) By Vote of 13–0–2," July 30, 2004.
70. Ibid.
71. Mamdani, *Saviors and Survivors: Darfur*, p. 221.
72. Ibid., p. 69.
73. De Waal and Flint, *Darfur*, p. 41.
74. Mamdani, p. 104.
75. UN CAD Nyala, "Meeting with Mohamed Hamdan (Hameti) in Nyala," March 4, 2008.
76. Ibid.

77. Mamdani, p. 6.
78. IRIN News Network, 2003.
79. E.g., BBC News, "Sudan's shadowy Arab militia," April 10, 2004.
80. Email correspondence with Alex de Waal, March 5, 2008.
81. UN CAD Nyala.
82. E.g., *Unreported World*, "Meet the Janjaweed," Channel 4, March 14 2008.
83. Hilal, Musa, author interview, Omdurman, Sudan, November 16, 2007.
84. He is repeatedly reported to have done so elsewhere—see Prunier, *Darfur*, p. 45.
85. Hilal, op. cit.
86. Mamdani, p. 300.
87. Haggar, "The Origins and Organization of the Janjawiid in Darfur," 2007.
88. Ibid.
89. De Waal and Flint, p. 36.
90. Lewis, *A Modern History of the Somali*, pp. 217–218.
91. Kaldor, *New and Old Wars*, p. 22.
92. Ibid., p. 98.
93. Ibid., pp. 117–18.

4. ECONOMIES OF MOVEMENT

1. Fonseca, *Bury Me Standing*.
2. Buckley, Stephen, "Nomads by Choice," *The Washington Post*, December 8, 1996, p. A01.
3. USAID Staff, author interviews, Ulaanbaatar, Mongolia, October, 2012.
4. Fischer, Anja, "Research and Nomads in the Age of Globalization," *Tuareg Society Within a Globalized World*, London: IB Tauris, 2010, p. 11.
5. See, for example, the "Tuareg Volkswagen," or the photograph of a Mursi tribesman with an iPod, originating at "iLounge," made famous by *Wired* magazine in 2007.
6. Ibid., p. 17.
7. Ibid.
8. Scholze, Marko, "Between the Worlds: Tuareg as Entrepreneurs in Tourism," in Fischer, op. cit.
9. Ibid.
10. Little, *Somalia*, p. xv.
11. Garad, Ismail Mohamad, author interview, Garissa, Kenya, January 2011.
12. Little, pp. 37–38.
13. Davies, Jonathan and Richard Hatfield, "The Economics of Mobile Pastoralism: A Global Summary," *Nomadic Peoples Journal*, Volume 11, Issue 1, 2007.

14. Hesse and MacGregor, J., *Pastoralism: Drylands' Hidden Asset? Developing a Framework for Assessing the Value of Pastoralism in East Africa*, International Institute for Environment and Development (IIED) 142, 2006.

15. Ibid., p. 15; emphasis mine.

16. Ibid., p. 16.

17. Others have come to similar conclusions through different methods. See Irons, William, and Neville Dyson-Hudson (eds), op. cit.

18. Ibid., see conclusion.

19. Poulton and ag Youssef, p. 49.

20. Youssef, Ibrahim ag, author interviews, Kutum, Sudan, November, 2007.

21. "Targui" is a Francophone synonym for Tuareg/Touareg.

22. As reported by Poulton and Youssef, pp. 41–42.

23. Davies and Hatfield, p. 1.

24. Scheele, *Smugglers and Saints of the Sahara*, p. 122.

25. See chapter 1.

26. E.g.: ibid., p. 12: "Rather than as a town, al-Khalil is thus perhaps best understood as a truck-stop: as a node in various overlapping networks that derive their power and standing from the outside, and that have little to do with each other."

27. Ibid., pp. 15–16.

28. Poulton and Youssef, p. 25.

29. Scheele, p. 23: "As to the trader…he entrusts the *badawi* [people of the desert] with some necessary goods. Then comes the man from the customs and by force collects duties (*khallām al-diwāna*) on what is not the *badawī's* property, and on all his valuables although …. And this does not only happen to one but it happens to many, and this stops the trader from trading with the people of the desert."

30. Ibid., p. 132.

31. Associated Press, "Sahara new centre for drugs trading, UN warns," *The Guardian*, December 9, 2009.

32. UNODC, *World Drug Report 2009*, New York: United Nations, 2009.

33. Scheele, p. 132.

34. Ibid., p. 132.

35. For another excellent relationship between nomadic identity and economic development, see for example Chatty, *From Camel to Truck*.

36. Scheele, p. 131.

37. Ibid., p. 306.

38. Long, Simon, "Mine, all Mine," *The Economist*, January 21, 2012.

39. Fortune Staff, "Global 500," *Fortune*, 2011. http://money.cnn.com/magazines/fortune/global500/2011/snapshots/11028.html

40. Macalister, Terry, "Ethical business: Norway ejects mining giant Rio from its pension portfolio," *The Guardian*, September 9, 2008.

41. Campbell, Duncan, "Mining accused of complicity in rights violations," *The Guardian*, November 20, 2007.

42. E.g., Oyu Tolgoi Watch, *Oyu Tolgoi Copper-Gold-Silver Mine, South Gobi, Mongolia*. April 12, 2011. http://www.miningwatch.ca/sites/miningwatch.ca/f iles/OT_issues.pdf

43. Administrator, "Australian Mining Giants to Deprive Mongolians of Way of Life?" *Love Perth*, January 31, 2012. http://www.loveperth.com.au/this-that/australian-mining-giants-to-deprive-mongolians-of-way-of-life/ Emphasis mine.

44. Rio Tinto International Media Tour, author interview, Oyu Tolgoi, Mongolia, September 2011.

45. McRae, Cameron, "Halfway There" Speech, Oyu Tolgoi: September 25, 2012.

46. Gaardi, Badruun, author interview, Ulaanbaatar, Mongolia, October, 2011.

47. E.g., Palma, "Dependency and Development".

48. Rio Tinto, *Why cultural heritage matters: A resource guide for integrating cultural heritage management into Communities work at Rio Tinto*, London: Rio Tinto, 2011.

49. Toya and family, author interview, near Oyu Tolgoi, Mongolia, September 23, 2011.

50. Hill, Christina, Serena Lillywhite and Michael Simon, *Guide to Free and Prior Consent*, Victoria: Oxfam, 2010.

51. United Nations General Assembly, *United Nations Declaration on The Rights of Indigenous Peoples*, See Article 32(2).

52. Rio Tinto, *Communities Standard 2011*, Prepared by Bruce Harvey, authorized by Rio Tinto ExCo, London: Rio Tinto, 2011, p. 17.

53. Toya interview, op. cit.

54. See for example, Rio Tinto, *Response to OT Watch and RAID regarding development plans for the Oyu Tolgoi mining complex in Mongolia*, May 18, 2010.

55. For more on this see chapter 1 on property rights.

56. Rio/OT deny accusations of forced relocation. Rio Tinto, op. cit., May 2010.

57. Ibid., p. 1.

58. Tseren, Nadmid, author interview, Ulaanbaatar, Mongolia, September, 2011.

59. Ibid.

60. This incident was corroborated by another source at Rio Tinto, and while the nomads she spoke with were not interviewed for this book, others in the area confirmed the story's plausibility.

61. Elbegdorj, T., Remarks to the Oxford Union, October 25, 2011.

62. McRae, op. cit.

63. Including: Dan Boren of Oklahoma, Jo Bonner of Alabama, Dave Camp of Michigan, Tom Latham of Iowa, and Greg Walden of Oregon.

64. US Embassy, Ulaanbaatar, *Summary of High Level Meetings during Codel Boehner*. August 13, 2009 via Wikileaks. Ref # 220601, "09ULAANBAATAR236".

65. Ibid., p. 1.

66. US Embassy, Ulaanbaatar, *Mongolia Scenesetter for Codel Boehner*, July 30, 2009 via Wikileaks. Ref # 218695, "09ULAANBAATAR208": "For U.S. commercial interests such as mining firms Peabody Energy and Rio Tinto and equipment makers Caterpillar, Ingersoll-Rand, Bucyrus, and John Deere, mining is THE industry that will provide the income necessary to ensure long-term purchases of U.S. goods and services. Failure to move on the Rio Tinto/ Ivanhoe Oyu Tolgoi copper-gold project has already cost U.S. export interests an estimated USD 200 million in equipment sales and other contracts. Separately, the Embassy is providing advocacy support for Peabody to secure the operating rights for the major Tavan Tolgoi coking coal deposit." See chapter 5 for discussion of one representative group, Tsetsegee Munkhbayar's "Fire Nation."

68. Agrawal, *Greener Pastures*, 1999.

69. Ibid., p. 112.

70. Ibid., p. 122.

5. THE CLIMATE OF THE COMMONS

1. Harris, R.B., "Rangeland degradation on the Qinghai-Tibetan plateau: A review of the evidence of its magnitude and causes," *Journal of Arid Environments*, No. 74, 2010, p. 1. N.B. "Pastoralism is also the dominant land-use in the other major biomes of western China (e.g., Mongolian Plateau, Tarim, and Dzungarian Basins), as well as in adjacent Mongolia, Kazakhstan, Kyrgyzstan, and Tajikistan...."

2. Ibid.

3. McCay, B., and Acheson, J., "Human ecology of the commons" in McCay, B., and Acheson, J. (eds), *The Question of the Commons*, Tucson: University of Arizona Press, 1987, p. 3.

4. Luterbacher, Urs, and Detlef Sprinz, "Problems of Global Environmental Cooperation," in *International Relations and Global Climate Change*, London: The MIT Press, 2001, p. 7.

5. Ibid., p. 7.

6. Ibid., p. 6.

7. Benanav, Michael, "Is there room for India's Nomads?," *Christian Science Monitor*, July 31, 2009.

8. Barfield, 1981.

9. See for example, Foggin, Marc, "Rethinking 'Ecological Migration' and the Value of Cultural Continuity: A Response to Wang, Song, and Hu," *AMBIO A Journal of the Human Environment*, November 2010.

10. McCabe, J. Terrence, "Turkana Pastoralism: A Case Against the Tragedy of the Commons," *Human Ecology*, Vol. 18, No. 1, 1990, p. 82.

11. Ibid., p. 83.

12. Benanav, op. cit.

13. See Harris in next sub-section on China, or for another good example: Williams, Dee Mack, *Beyond Great Walls: environment, identity, and development on the Chinese grasslands of Inner Mongolia*, Stanford: Stanford University Press, 2002.

14. Hardin, Garret, "Extensions of the Tragedy of the Commons," *Science*, Vol. 280, no. 5364, 1 May, 1998: pp. 682–683.

15. Luterbacher, chapter 1: "Although the greenhouse warming theory was put forward more than a century ago by the Swedish chemist Svante Arrehnius (1896) climate change did not emerge as a *political...* until the 1990s."

16. McCabe, p. 82.

17. Rao, Aparna, "Pastoral Nomads, the State and the Dachigam National Park in Kashmir," *Nomadic Peoples Journal*, Vol. 6, No. 2, 2002, p. 72.

18. Ibid., p. 77.

19. Harris, op. cit., p. 3.

20. See chapter 4.

21. Ramban, W.P., *Revised Working Plan for the Ramban Forest Division 1961/62 to 1971/72*. Government of Jammu and Kashmir. 1961. Quoted in Rao, p. 76.

22. US Consulate, Chengdu. *Tibetan Nomad Policies In Sichuan: Settlement, Conflict And Authority*. January 8, 2010 via Wikileaks. Ref # 242869, 10CHENGDU8.

23. Ibid.

24. Harris, p. 7.

25. Ibid., p. 7.

26. Ibid., p. 2.

27. Ibid., p. 6. One example: Zhou, H.K., Zhao, X.Q., Tang, Y.H., Gu, S., Zhou, L., "Alpine grassland degradation and its control in the source region of the Yangtze and Yellow Rivers, China," *Grassland Science*, No. 51, 2005, pp. 191–203.

28. Ibid., p. 6.

29. Associated Press, "Tibet Unrest Spreads into Neighbouring Provinces," *The Guardian*, March 16, 2008.

30. US Consulate, Chengdu, op. cit., January 8, 2010.

31. Ibid.

32. Howerton, Hart and A.R.E. Sinclair, "Maximizing the Economy of the Serengeti National Park through Conservation," Project Report prepared for Frankfurt Zoological Society by Economics Research Associates HKLM, September, 2007.

33. US Consulate, Chengdu, *Tibetan Herders In Sichuan's Hongyuan County Face*

Uncertain Future As County Develops, January 11, 2010, via Wikileaks. Ref # 243033, 10CHENGDU9.

34. US Consulate, Chengdu, op. cit., January 8, 2010.

35. Fisher, Elanore, "Forced Re-settlement, Rural Livelihoods and Wildlife Conservation along the Ugalla River in Tanzania," in Chatty, 2002.

36. Enghoff, Martin, "Wildlife Conservation, Ecological Strategies, and Pastoral Communities," *Nomadic Peoples Journal*, No. 25, 1990.

37. Atlaf, Sana, "Kashmir Conflict Spares Wildlife," *The Guardian*, June 16, 2011.

38. Lawrence quoted in Rao, p. 83.

39. Galvin, Kathleen, et. al. "Compatibility of Pastoralism and Conservation" in Chatty, 2002, p. 37.

40. Ibid., p. 50.

41. Ibid.

42. Ibid., p. 40.

43. Ibid., p. 39.

44. Ibid., p. 55.

45. Raustiala, Kal, "Nonstate Actors in the Global Climate Regime" in Luterbacher, op. cit., p. 115.

46. *Guardian* staff, "On the Move," *The Guardian*, May 29, 2002.

47. WISP Staff, "How We Work," IUCN.org

48. Raustiala, p. 115. Emphasis mine.

49. Partially explaining why large, more successful NGOs like the WWF, for example, tend not to address the nomadic situation.

50. Dana Committee, *Main Page*, http://www.danadeclaration.org/.

51. Dana Committee, *The Dana Declaration On Mobile Peoples and Conservation*. danadeclaration.org

52. US Consulate, Chengdu, *Nomadic Resettlement And The New Socialist Countryside In Sichuan Province's Aba Prefecture*, June 4, 2007 via Wikileaks. Ref # 110694, 07CHENGDU140.

53. Poulton and Youssef, p. 48.

54. Lapinski, Valerie, "Showcase: Travelling with the Van Gujjar Tribe, *The New York Times.com*, October 7, 2009.

55. Rao, p. 76.

56. BBC News, "Swazi awarded for poacher murder expose," *BBC News*, April 19, 2010.

57. Goldman Foundation, "About Us." *Goldmanprize.org*.

58. Ibid., "Award Citation."

59. National Geographic Staff, "Explorers-Bios Tsetsegee Munkhbayar," *National Geographic.com*.

60. Boyonbat, author interview, Central Onggi River, Mongolia, October 2011.

61. Jamyansaren, author interview, Near Bayanzag, Mongolia, October 2011.

62. Ibid.

63. Dawaa, author interview, south of Ulaanbaatar, Mongolia, October 2011.

64. Tsetserlee, author interview, south of Ulaanbaatar, Mongolia, October 2011. E.g.: "Our governor is corrupt. We say, are you also bribed? They have no response for that."

65. Transparency International, "Corruption Perception Index 2011," Transparency. org.

66. Munkhbayar.

67. See chapter 4, conclusion.

68. US Consulate, Chengdu, op. cit., January 11, 2010.

69. Nature officer near Three Camels Lodge, author interview, Mongolia, October 2011.

70. Jamyansaren, op. cit.

71. In addition, this binary suggests mutual exclusivity.

72. Goldman Foundation, op. cit.

73. Kohn, Michael, "Mongolia herder on mission to tackle mining firms," *Tengri News*, June 8, 2011.

74. Bloomberg Staff, "Mineral-Rich, People-Poor Mongolia Prepares for Flood of Money Next Decade," *Bloomberg News*, July 21, 2011.

75. Huhung, op. cit.

76. Rao, p. 72.

77. Huhung, October 2011.

78. Chatty.

79. Tsetsegee Munkhbayar, author interview, Ulaanbaatar, Mongolia, September 2011.

6. SUMMATION AND THE AGENTIC QUESTION

1. Chapter 4, pp. 142–149.

2. International Crisis Group, "Crisis Watch No. 102–105," Brussels: International Crisis Group, February–May, 2012.

3. E.g. contradictions within the *hakura* system of land ownership, see de Waal and Flint 2008, for more on this.

4. Darfur-Darfur Dialogue and Reconciliation Team, author interviews, Sudan, 2007.

5. Khelifi, Oualid, "Mali: What is Really Happening," *Ceasefire Magazine*, April 9, 2012.

6. Youssef, Ibrahim, email correspondence, April 7, 2012.

7. Youssef, Ibrahim, email correspondence, April 11, 2012.

8. Hazareesingh, Sudhir, author interview, Oxford, May 29, 2012.

9. Bussow.

10. BBC News, "Saharan Musicians win Uncut Award," *BBC News*, November 9, 2009.

11. Krateli, Saverio, "Education Provisio to Nomadic Pastoralists: A Literature Review," IDS Working Paper 126, London: Institute for Development Studies, 2001.

12. The Global Gathering of Pastoralists, "Recommendations," Author Observation, Nairobi: December, 2013.

13. Pettit, Philip, "Collective Intentions" in Naffine, Owens and Williams (eds), *Intention in Law and Philosophy*, London: Ashgate, 2001.

14. Bratman, Michael, "Agency, Time, and Sociality," Presidential Address delivered before the Eighty-Fourth Annual Pacific Division Meeting of The American Philosophical Association, San Francisco: 2010.

15. Velleman, David, "How To Share an Intention," *Philosophy and Phenomenological Research*, Vol. 57, No. 1, March 1997, pp. 29–50.

16. Honneth, Axel, *The Struggle for Recognition: The Moral Grammar of Social Conflicts*, Cambridge: The MIT Press, 1996, p. 163.

17. Ibid.

18. Ibid., p. 166.

19. Honneth's examples are "spontaneous revolts, organized strikes," and "passive forms of resistance"—all three of which are seen in nomadism.

20. Ibid., p. 168.

REFERENCES

African Union, Department of Rural Economy and Agriculture, *Pastoral Policy Framework in Africa: Securing, Protecting and Improving Lives, Livelihoods and Rights of Pastoralist Communities*, Addis Ababa, 2010.

Agrawal, Arun, *Greener Pastures: Politics, Markets, and Community Among a Migrant Pastoral People*, Durham: Duke University Press, 1999.

Andaya, Barbara, *A History of Malaysia*, London: Palgrave Macmillan, 1984.

———, *The Installation of the First Sultan of Selangor in 1776*, MBRAS: 1974.

Andaya, Leonard, "The Structure of Power in Seventeenth-Century Johor" in Anthony Reid and Lance Castle (eds) *Pre Colonial State Systems in Southeast Asia: The Malay peninsula, Sumatra, Bali-Lombok, South Celebes*, Monographs of the Malaysian Branch of the Royal Asiatic Society, 1974, p. 7.

Arberry, A.J., trans. *The Koran*, New York: Macmillan, 1986.

Areddy, James, 'Mining Boom Fuels New Mongol Hoard,' *The Wall Street Journal*, http://online.wsj.com/article/SB1000142405 2748703421204576331144234070656.html; Accessed August 16, 2011.

Associated Press, "Sahara new centre for drugs trading, UN warns," *The Guardian*, December 9, 2009, http://www.guardian.co.uk/world/2009/dec/09/sahara-drugs-trade-heroin-cocaine

———, "Amnesty: Imported Arms Fueling Darfur Conflict" *ABC News*, February 9, 2012, http://abcnews.go.com/US/wireStory/amnesty-imported-arms-fueling-darfur-conflict-15543171#.T0Ofz3IzUVk

———, "Tibet unrest spreads into neighbouring provinces," *The Guardian*, March 16 2008, http://www.guardian.co.uk/world/2008/mar/16/tibet.china1

Atlaf, Sana, "Kashmir Conflict Spares Wildlife," *The Guardian*, June 16, 2011.

Austen, Ralph, *Trans Saharan Africa in World History*, Oxford: Oxford University Press, 2010.

Azarya, Victor, *Nomads and the state in Africa: the political roots of marginality*, Rijksuniversiteit te Leiden, Afrika-Studiecentrum, Leiden: 1996.

REFERENCES

Baldwin, David, 'Power and International Relations,' *Handbook of International Relations*, London: Sage Publications, 2002.

Baran, Paul A., "Discussion," *The American Economic Review*, Vol. 41, No. 2, Papers and Proceedings of the Sixty-third Annual Meeting of the American Economic Association, May, 1951, pp. 355–358.

Barfield, Thomas, *The Central Asian Arabs of Afghanistan*, Austin: University of Texas Press, 1981.

———, *The Nomadic Alternative*, London: Prentice Hall International, 1993.

———, *The Perilous Frontier: Nomadic Empires and China, 221 BC to AD 1757*, Oxford: Blackwell, 1992.

Barth, Frederik, *The Nomads of South Persia*, Boston: Little Brown, 1961.

Bates, Daniel and Susan Lees, 'The Origins of Specialized Nomadic Pastoralism: A Systemic Model,' *American Antiquity* Vol. 39, No. 2, April 1974.

Bautman, Elif, "The Sanctuary: the world's oldest temple and the dawn of civilization," *The New Yorker*, Vol. 87, No. 41, December 2011.

Baylis, John, Steve Smith and Patricia Owens, *The Globalization of World Politics*, Oxford: Oxford University Press, 2011.

BBC News, "Q&A: Ethiopia's Afar Region," *BBC News*, January 18, 2012, http://www.bbc.co.uk/news/world-africa-16620783

———, "Saharan Musicians win Uncut Award," *BBC News*, November 9, 2009, http://news.bbc.co.uk/1/hi/8349904.stm

———, Sudan's shadowy Arab militia *BBC News*, April 10, 2004, http://news.bbc.co.uk/1/hi/world/africa/3613953.stm

———, "Swazi awarded for poacher murder expose," *BBC News*, April 19, 2010. http://news.bbc.co.uk/1/hi/world/africa/8630021.stm

Benanav, Michael, "Is there room for India's Nomads?" *Christian Science Monitor*, July 31, 2009. http://www.csmonitor.com/World/Asia-South-Central/2009/0731/p17s07-wosc.html/(page)/2

Blench, Roger, "You Can't Go Home Again: Pastoralism in the new Millenium," London: Overseas Development Institute, May 2001.

Bloomberg Staff, "Mineral-Rich, People-Poor Mongolia Prepares for Flood of Money Next Decade," *Bloomberg News*, July 21, 2011, http://www.bloomberg.com/news/2011-07-21/mineral-rich-people-poor-mongolia-prepares-for-flood-of-money.html

Bocco, Riccardo, "International organisations ad the settlement of nomads in the Arab Middle East, 1950–1990," in Mundy, Martha and Basim Musallam (eds), *The Transformation of Nomadic Society in the Arab East*, Cambridge: Cambridge University Press, 2000.

Bodansky, James, "History of the Global Climate Change Regime," in Luterbacher, Urs, and Detlef Sprinz, (eds), *International Relations and Global Climate Change*, Cambridge: The MIT Press, 2001.

REFERENCES

Booth, Ken, "Critical Explorations," *Critical Security Studies and World Politics*, London: Lynne Reinner, 2005.

Boyonbat, Author Interview, Central Onggi River, Mongolia, October 2011.

Bratman, Michael, "Agency, Time, and Sociality," Presidential Address delivered before the Eighty-Fourth Annual Pacific Division Meeting of The American Philosophical Association, San Francisco: 2010.

Brewer, Anthony, "Adam Smith's Stages of History" Discussion Paper No. 08/601, Department of Economics, University of Bristol, 2008.

Brody, Hugh, *Maps & Dreams: Indians and the British Columbia Frontier*, Long Grove: Waveland Press, 1993.

Buckley, Stephen, "Nomads by Choice," *The Washington Post*, Sunday, December 8, 1996; Page A01 http://www.washingtonpost.com/wp-srv/inatl/longterm/nomads/nomad_1.htm

Bull, Hedley, *The Anarchical Society: A Study of Order in World Politics*, London: Palgrave Macmillan, 2002.

Bussow, Johann, "Bedouin Historiography in the Making: And Indigenous History of the Hasana Tribe in Syria," *Nomadismus in der 'Alten Welt*,' Berlin: LIT Verlag Munster, 2012.

Buzan, Barry, and Richard Little, *International Systems in World History*, Oxford: Oxford University Press, 2000.

Campbell, Duncan, "Mining accused of complicity in rights violations," *The Guardian*, November 20, 2007, http://www.guardian.co.uk/business/2007/nov/20/mining.riotinto

Cardoso, Fernando Henrique, and Enzo Faleto, *Dependency and Development in Latin America*, Berkeley: University of California Press, 1979.

Chatty, Dawn, Author Interview, Oxford, UK, December 12, 2011.

———, *From Camel to Truck: The Bedouin in the Modern World*, London, Vantage, 1986.

———, "The Bedouin in Contemporary Syria: The Persistence of Tribal Authority and Control," *The Middle East Journal*, Vol. 64, 2010.

Chatty, Dawn, and Marcus Colchester, *Conservation and Mobile Indigenous Peoples: Displacement, Forced Settlement, and Sustainable Development*, Oxford: Berghahn Books, 2002.

Chatwin, Bruce, *Anatomy of Restlessness*, London: Picador, 1997.

Chou, Cynthia, *The Orang Suku Laut of Riau, Indonesia: The Inalienable Gift of Territory*, Abingdon: Routledge, 2010.

Chi'en, Ssu-Ma-, *Records of the Grand Historian of China, trans. Bruce Watson*, New York: Columbia University Press, 1961.

Clastres, Pierre, *Society Against the State*, trans by Robert Hurley, Oxford: Basil Blackwell, 1977.

Cox, R.W., "Social Forces, States, and World Orders: Beyond International Relations Theory," *Millennium*, Vol. 10 (2), 1981.

REFERENCES

Crilly, Rob, "'Peacekeeping' a struggle in Sudan," *USA Today*, November 30, 2005, http://www.usatoday.com/news/world/2005-11-29-african-union-sudan_x.htm

Dana Committee, *The Dana Declaration On Mobile Peoples and Conservation*, http://www.danadeclaration.org/main_declarationenglish.shtml

Davies, Jonathan and Richard Hatfield, "The Economics of Mobile Pastoralism: A Global Summary," *Nomadic Peoples Journal*, Volume 11, Issue 1, 2007.

Dawaa, Author Interview, South of Ulaanbaatar, Mongolia, October 2011.

Darfur-Darfur Dialogue and Reconciliation Team, Author Interviews, Darfur, Sudan, December 2007.

De Waal, Alex, "Counter-Insurgency on the Cheap," *The London Review of Books*, Vol. 26, No. 15. August 5, 2004, pp. 25–27. http://www.lrb.co.uk/v26/n15/alex-de-waal/counter-insurgency-on-the-cheap

De Waal, Alex and Julie Flint, *Darfur: A New History of a Long War*, London: Zed Press, 2008.

Deleuze, Gilles, and Félix Guattari, *A Thousand Plateaus: Capitalism and Schizophrenia* trans, Brian Massumi, London: Continuum, 2004.

Department of International Development, University of Oxford, *Refugee Studies Center Report: Mobile Indigenous Peoples Participations at the IUCN World Conservation Congress and the Human Rights Workshop October 1, 2008—October 9, 2008.*

Dovi, Suzanne, "Political Representation", *The Stanford Encyclopedia of Philosophy* (Fall 2011 Edition), Edward N. Zalta (ed.), forthcoming URL = <http://plato.stanford.edu/archives/fall2011/entries/political-representation/>

Dyer, Caroline, ed., *The Education of Nomadic Peoples: Current Issues, Future Prospects*, New York: Berghan Books, 2006.

Elbegdorj, T., Remarks to the Oxford Union, October 25, 2011.

Elphinstone, W. G., "The Future of the Bedouin of Northern Arabia" *International Affairs* (Royal Institute of International Affairs 1944–), Vol. 21, No. 3, July 1945.

Ethiopian Review, "Why Did TPLF Blamed [sic] Eritrea on ARDUF Operation?" http://www.ethiopianreview.com/forum/viewtopic.php?f=2&t=35280

Evans-Pritchard, E. E., *The Nuer: A description of the modes of livelihood and political institutions of a Nilotic people*, Oxford: Oxford University Press, 1968.

Fanon, Franz, *The Wretched of the Earth*, trans. Richard Philcox, New York: Grove Press, 1994.

Fisher, Anja, "Research and Nomads in the Age of Globalization," *Tuareg Society Within a Globalized World*, London: Tarius Academic Studies, 2010, p. 11.

Fisher, Eleanor, "Forced Re-settlement, Rural Livelihoods and Wildlife Conservation along the Ugalla River in Tanzania," in Chatty, Dawn, and Marcus Colchester, *Conservation and Mobile Indigenous Peoples: Displacement, Forced Settlement, and Sustainable Development*, Oxford: Berghahn Books, 2002.

Flockhart, Trine, 'Complex Socialization: A Framework for the Study of State Socialization,' *European Journal of International Relations*, Vol. 12, Issue 1, March 2006.

Foggin, Marc, "Rethinking 'Ecological Migration' and the Value of Cultural Continuity: A Response to Wang, Song, and Hu," *AMBIO A Journal of the Human Environment*, November 2010.

Fortune Staff, "The Global 500," *Fortune* 2011. http://money.cnn.com/magazines/fortune/global500/2011/snapshots/11028.html

Fox News, "Sudanese army attacks South Darfur village," December 11, 2010. http://www.foxnews.com/world/2010/12/11/sudans-army-attacks-south-darfur-village/

Gaardi, Badruun, Author Interviews, Ulaanbaatar, Mongolia, October, 2011.

Garad, Ismail Mohamad, Author Interview, Garissa, Kenya, January 2011.

General Conference of the International Labour Organization, *Convention concerning Indigenous and Tribal Peoples in Independent Countries*, Geneva, May 9, 1991.

Gellner, Ernest, *State & Society in Soviet Thought*, Oxford: Basil Blackwell, 1988.

Gilbert, Jérémie, "Nomadic Territories: A Human Rights Approach to Nomadic Peoples' Land Rights," *Human Rights Law Review*, Volume 7, Issue 4, 2007.

Glubb, John B., "The Bedouins of Northern Arabia" *Royal Central Asian Journal*, vol. XXII, part I, 1935, p. 13.

———, *Handbook of the Nomads, Semi-Nomads, Semi-Sedentary Tribes of Syria*, GSI Headquarters, 9th Army, 1942.

Goldman Foundation, "About Us," http://www.goldmanprize.org/aboutus/founders

———, "Award Citation" Goldmanprize.org http://www.goldmanprize.org/node/606

Guardian Staff, "On the Move," *The Guardian*, May 29, 2002. http://www.danadeclaration.org/pdf/mediaenglish3.pdf.

Haggar, Ali, "The origins and Organization of the Janjawiid in Darfur," in *War in Darfur and the Search for Peace*, London: Justice Africa, 2007.

Hannoum, Abdelmajid, 'Translation And The Colonial Imaginary: Ibn Khaldûn Orientalist,' *History and Theory*, No. 42, February 2003.

Hardin, Garret, "Extensions of the Tragedy of the Commons," *Science* Vol. 280 no. 5364, May 1, 1998: pp. 682–683.

Harmon Stephen, "From GSPC to AQIM: The Evolution of an Algerian Islamist Terrorist Group into an Al-Qa'ida Affiliate," *Concerned African Scholars*, Bulletin No. 85, Spring. 2010, Concernedafricanscholars.org

Harris, R.B., "Rangeland degradation on the Qinghai-Tibetan plateau: A review of the evidence of its magnitude and causes," *Journal of Arid Environments*, No. 74, 2010.

Hauslohner, Abigail, "Bedouin Rising: Egypt's Wild Frontier Tries to Get an

REFERENCES

American Audience," *TIME,* March 15, 2012, http://www.time.com/time/world/article/0,8599,2109204,00.html#ixzz1pGqhvoB4

Hazaristan Times, "Protests in Italy Against Kuchi Attacks in Hazarajat," June 13, 2010, http://hazaristantimes.wordpress.com/2010/06/13/protest-in-italy-against-kuchi-attacks-in-hazarajat/

Heredia, Rudolf, and Shereen Ratnagar (eds), *Mobile and Marginalized Peoples: Perspectives from the Past,* New Delhi: Manohar, 2003.

Herodotus, *The Histories,* Trans. Aubrye de Selincourt, London: Penguin, 1996.

Hesse, C., and MacGregor, J., *Pastoralism: Drylands' Hidden Asset? Developing a Framework for Assessing the Value of Pastoralism in East Africa,* International Institute for Environment and Development (IIED) 142, 2006.

Hilal, Musa, Author Interview, Omdurman, Sudan, November 16, 2007.

Hill, Christina, Serena Lillywhite and Michael Simon, *Guide to Free and Prior Consent,* Victoria: Oxfam Australia, 2010.

Honneth, Axel. *The Struggle for Recognition: The Moral Grammar of Social Conflicts.* Cambridge: The MIT Press, 1996.

Howitt, Richard, *Resources, Nations and Indigenous Peoples: Case Studies from Australasia, Melanesia, and Southeast Asia,* Oxford: Oxford University Press, 1996.

Huhung and family, Author Interview, North of Tavan Tolgoi, Mongolia, September 26, 2011.

Human Rights Watch, *Darfur Bleeds: Recent Cross Border Violence in Chad,* New York: HRW Report. February, 2006.

———, "Massacres of Hazaras in Afghanistan," February, 2001. Http://www.hrw.org/legacy/reports/2001/afghanistan/

Khaldun, Ibn, *The Muqaddimah: an Introduction to History,* trans. Franz Rosenthal, Princeton: Princeton University Press, 1989.

Ifeka, Caroline, "War on 'Terror': AFRICOM, the Kleptocratic State and Under-Class Militancy in West Africa-Nigeria." *Concerned African Scholars,* Bulletin No. 85, Spring, 2010. Concernedafricanscholars.org

Inkeles, Alex, 'Social Structure and Socialization' in *Handbook of Socialisation Theory and Research,* David Doslin (ed.), Chicago: Rand McNally, 1969.

Isidoros, Konstantina. "Western Sahara and the United States' Geographical Imaginings." *Concerned African Scholars,* Bulletin No. 85, Spring. 2010. Concernedafricanscholars.org

Integrated Regional Information Networks (IRIN), "Afghanistan: Threat of ethnic clashes over grazing land," UN Office for the Coordination of Humanitarian Affairs. April 7, 2008. http://www.irinnews.org/Report.aspx?ReportId=77647

———, "The Escalating Crisis in Darfur," Nairobi: UN Office for the Coordination of Humanitarian Affairs, December 31, 2003.

International Committee of the Red Cross. *Protocol Additional to the Geneva*

REFERENCES

Conventions of 12 August 1949, and relating to the Protection of Victims of International Armed Conflicts (Protocol I). Geneva, June 8, 1977. Article 1, section 4.

International Crisis Group, "Crisis Watch No. 102–105", Brussels: International Crisis Group, February–May, 2012.

Irons, William, and Neville Dyson-Hudson (eds), *Perspectives on Nomadism*, Leiden: E.J. Brill, 1972.

Jamyansaren, Author Interview, Near Bayanzag, Mongolia, October 2011.

Kahl, Colin H, "COIN of the Realm Is There a Future for Counterinsurgency?" *Foreign Affairs*, November/December 2007.

Kahner, Leander, "Mursi Tribeswoman with iPod and AK-47," *Wired.com*. April 22, 2007. http://www.wired.com/cult_of_mac/2007/04/mursi_tribeswom/

Kaldor, Mary, *New and Old Wars: Organized Violenece in a Global Era*, Stanford: Stanford University Press, 2007.

Kant, Immanuel, *Political Writings*, trans. Hans Siegbert Reiss, Cambridge: Cambridge University Press, 1991.

Keenan, Jeremy, "Al Qaeda in the Sahel," *Al-Jazeera.com* August 29, 2010. http://www.aljazeera.com/focus/2010/07/201071994556568918.html

Khazanov, A. M., *Nomads and the Outside World*, trans. Julia Crookenden, Cambridge: Cambridge University Press, 1984.

———, 'Pastoralists in the 'Age of Globalization,': Challenges of the 21st Century, *Dialogue Between Cultures and Civilizations: Present State and Perspectives of Nomadism in a Globalizing World, Proceedings of the International Conference*, Jorg Janzen and Batboldyn Enkhtuvshin (eds),. Ulaanbaatar, August 9–14, 2004.

Khazanov, A.M., and J, Ginat (eds). *Changing Nomads in a Changing World*, Sussex: Sussex Academic Press, 1974.

Khelifi, Oualid, "Mali: What is Really Happening," *Ceasefire Magazine*, April 9, 2012. http://ceasefiremagazine.co.uk/mali/

Khoury, Philip, and Joseph Kostiner, (eds), *Tribes and State Formation in The Middle East*, London: IB Tauris, 1991.

Kilcullen, David, *The Accidental Guerrilla: Fighting Small Wars in the Midst of a Big One*, London: Hurst, 2009.

Kingsbury, Benedict, "'Indigenous Peoples" in International Law: A Constructivist Approach to the Asian Controversy,' *The Concept of Indigenous Peoples in Asia: A Resource Book*, Christian Erni (ed.), IWGIA Document No. 123: Copenhagen, 2008.

The King James Bible, New York: Oxford Edition: 1769; King James Bible Online, 2008.

Kohn, Michael, "Mongolia herder on mission to tackle mining firms," *Tengri News*, June 8, 2011.

Korda, Michael, *Hero: The Life and Legend of Lawrence of Arabia*, London: Harper Collins, 2011.

REFERENCES

Krasner, Stephen, *Organized Hypocrisy*, Princeton: Princeton University Press, 1999.

———, "State, Power, Anarchism: A Discussion on The Art of Not Being Governed: An Anarchist History of Upland Southeast Asia" *Perspectives on Politics*, March 2011.

Krateli, Saverio, "Education Provisio to Nomadic Pastoralists: A Literature Review," IDS Working Paper 126, London: Institute for Development Studies, 2001.

Lacey, Marc, "Leading Player in Darfur's Drama: The Hapless Camel," *The New York Times*, December 5, 2005, http://www.nytimes.com/2005/12/05/international/africa/05sudan.html

Lapinski, Valerie, "Showcase: Travelling with the Van Gujjar Tribe, *The New York Times.com*. October 7, 2009. http://lens.blogs.nytimes.com/2009/10/07/showcase-61/

Larotourrou, Paul, "Niger nomad speaks out: 'We are not terrorists!'" *France 24*, October 14, 2010. http://observers.france24.com/content/20101014-tuareg-perspective-stop-equating-people-aqmi-terrorists-mali-niger

Lattimore, Owen, *Inner Asian Frontiers of China*, New York: American Geographical Society, 1951.

———, *Studies in frontier history: collected papers, 1928–1958*, London: Oxford University Press, 1962.

Lawrence, T.E., *Seven Pillars of Wisdom*, Jonathan Cape: London, 1935.

Lebow, Richard, *The Tragic Vision of Politics: Ethics, Interests, and Orders*, Cambridge: Cambridge University press, 2003.

Lederer, Edith M, "UN Council feels heat for peace in Darfur," *The Boston Globe*, June 13, 2006. http://articles.boston.com/2006–06 13/news/29242561_1_african-union-arab-militias-sudanese

Lettola, Veli Pekka, *The Sami People: Traditions in Transition*, Fairbanks: Alaska University Press, 2004.

Lewis, I.M., *A Modern History of the Somali*, Oxford: James Currey, 2002.

Linklater, Andrew, "Political Community and Human Security," *Critical Security Studies and World Politics*, London: Lynne Reinner, 2005.

Little, Peter, *Somalia: Economy Without State*, Oxford: James Currey, 2003.

Locke, John, *Two Treatises of Government*, ed. Peter Laslett, Cambridge: Cambridge University Press, 1970.

Long, Simon, "Mine, all Mine," *The Economist*, January 21, 2012.

Luterbacher, Urs, and Detlef Sprinz, "Problems of Global Environmental Cooperation," in *International Relations and Global Climate Change*, London: The MIT Press, 2001.

Macalister, Terry, "Ethical business: Norway ejects mining giant Rio from its pension portfolio," *The Guardian*, September 9, 2008.

REFERENCES

Marcellinus, Ammianus, *The Later Roman Empire*, Penguin Books: London, 2004.

Mamdani, Mahmood, *Saviors and Survivors: Darfur, Politics, and the War on Terror*, Pantheon Books: New York, 2009.

McCabe, Terrence J., "Turkana Pastoralism: A Case Against the Tragedy of the Commons," *Human Ecology*, Vol. 18, No. 1, 1990.

McCay, B., and Acheson, J., "Human ecology of the commons" in McCay, B., and Acheson, J. (eds), *The Question of the Commons*, Tucson: University of Arizona Press, 1987.

McRae, Cameron, "Halfway There" Speech, Oyu Tolgoi: September 25, 2012.

Meir, Avinoam, "Nomads and the state: the spatial dynamics of centrifugal and Centripetal forces among the Israeli Negev Bedouin" *Political Geography Quarterly*, Volume 7, Issue 3, July 1988, pp. 251–270.

Mills, G., "Africa's new strategic significance," *The Washington Quarterly* Vol. 27, No. 4, 2004.

Molyneux, J.H., "The Simporna Expedition," *British North Borneo Herald*, 1902.

Mundy, Jacob, "Introduction: Securitizing the Sahara," *Concerned African Scholars*, Bulletin 85, Spring 2010. Concernedafricanscholars.org

National Geographic Staff, "Explorers-Bios Tsetsegee Munkhbayar," http://www.nationalgeographic.com/explorers/bios/tsetsegee-munkhbayar/ Accessed April 24, 2012.

The New York Times "Times Topics: Omar Hassan Al Bashir," July 14, 2011. http://topics.nytimes.com/top/reference/timestopics/people/b/omar_hassan_al_bashir/index.html

Nordstrom, Ester, *Tent Folk of the Far North*, trans. E. Gee Nash, London: Herbert Jenkins Limited, 1930.

Oyu Tolgoi Watch, *Oyu Tolgoi Copper-Gold-Silver Mine, South Gobi, Mongolia*. April 12, 2011. http://www.miningwatch.ca/sites/miningwatch.ca/f iles/OT_issues.pdf

Pace, Erik, "Owen Lattimore, Far East Scholar Accused by McCarthy, dies at 88". *The New York Times*. June 1, 1989. Retrived 1/12/11: http://www.nytimes.com/1989/06/01/obitu aries/owen-lattimore-far-east-scholar-accused-by-mccarthy-dies-at-88.html

Palma, Gabriel, "Dependency and Development: A Critical Overview", in Dudley Seers (ed.), *Dependency Theory: A Critical Reassessment*, London: Pinter, 1981.

Pettit, Philip, "Collective Intentions," in Naffine, Owens, and Williams, (eds). *Intention in Law and Philosophy*, London: Ashgate, 2001.

Pidd, Helen, "Background: The kidnapping of Edwin Dyer One of four Europeans seized in west African desert in January reported to have been beheaded by al-Qaida," *The Guardian*, June 3, 2009. http://www.guardian.co.uk/world/2009/jun/03/edwin-dyer-hostage-killed-al-qaida

REFERENCES

Pitkin, Hanna Fenichel, *The Concept of Representation*, London: University of California Press, 1967.

Pliny the Elder, *Natural History: A Selection*, John Healy, trans., Penguin Books: London, 1991.

Polk, William, *Passing Brave*, New York: Ballantine, 1973.

Poulton, Robin-Edward, and Youssef, Ibrahim ag, *A Peace of Timbuktu: Democratic Governance, Development and African Peacemaking*, Geneva: United Nations Institute for Disarmament Research, 1998.

Prunier, Gerard, *Darfur: The Ambiguous Genocide*, London: Hurst, 2007.

Rabinow, Paul (ed.), *The Foucault Reader*, London: Penguin Books, 1991.

Ragin, Charles C., and Howard S. Becker (eds), *What Is a Case?* Cambridge: Cambridge University Press, 2009.

Rao, Aparna, "Pastoral Nomads, the State and the Dachigam National Park in Kashmir," *Nomadic Peoples Journal*, Vol. 6, No. 2, 2002.

Rao, Aparna (ed.), *The Other Nomads*, Wein: Bohlau Verlag Kiln, 1987.

―――― and Michael Caisimir (eds), *Nomadism in South Asia*, New Delhi: Oxford University Press India, 2003.

Raustiala, Kal, "Nonstate Actors in the Global Climate Regime," In Luterbacher, Urs, and Detlef Sprinz (eds), *International Relations and Global Climate Change*, London: MIT Press, 2001, p. 115.

Reuters Africa, "Russian, Chinese arms used in Darfur abuse–Amnesty," Feb 9, 2012. http://af.reuters.com/article/commoditiesNews/idAFL5E8D76EN201 20209?sp=true Rio Tinto, *Communities Standard 2011*, Prepared by Bruce Harvey, authorized by Rio Tinto ExCo, Rio Tinto: London, 2011. www. riotinto.com/documents/ Communities_standard.pdf

―――――, *Response to OT Watch and RAID regarding development plans for the Oyu Tolgoi mining complex in Mongolia*, May 18, 2010.

―――――, *Why cultural heritage matters: A resource guide for integrating cultural heritage management into Communities work at Rio Tinto*, Rio Tinto: London, 2011, www. riotinto.com/documents/ReportsPublications/Rio_Tinto_Cultural_Heritage_Guide.pdf

Robertson-Smith, W., *Kinship and Marriage in Early Arabia*, Cambridge: Cambridge University Press, 1885.

Rosen, Lawrence, 'Theorizing from within: Ibn Khaldun and his Political Culture,' *Contemporary Sociology*, Vol. 34, No. 6, 2005.

Rosenberg, Justin, *The empire of civil society: a critique of the realist theory of international relations*, Verso: New York, 1994.

Said, Edward, 'Representing the Colonized: Anthropology's Interlocutors,' *Critical Inquiry*, Vol. 15, No. 2, 1989.

Salzman, Philip Carl,. *Pastoralists*, Boulder: Westview Press, 2004.

Salzman, Philip Carl and John Galaty (eds), *Nomads in a Changing World*, Naples: Istituto Universitario Orientale, 1990.

REFERENCES

Sather, Clifford, *The Bajau Laut: Adaptation, History, and Fate in a Maritime Fishing Society of South-eastern Sabah*, Oxford: Oxford University Press, 1997.

Scheele, Judith, *Smugglers and Saints of the Sahara: Regional Connectivity in the Twentieth Century*, Cambridge: Cambridge University Press, 2012.

Schmidt, Brian, 'Competing Realist Perceptions of Power,' *Millenium Journal of International Studies*, Volume 33, Number 3, 2005.

The Scotsman, "Darfur 'sliding into anarchy,'" 'November 5, 2005. http://www.scotsman.com/news/international/darfur_sliding_into_anarchy_1_1103153

Scott, James C., *The Art of Not Being Governed*, London: Yale University Press, 2009.

———, 'Hill and Valley in Southeast Asia…or Why the State is the Enemy of People who Move Around…or…Why Civilizations Can't Climb Hills,' *The Concept of Indigenous Peoples in Asia: A Resource Book*, Christian Erni (ed.), IWGIA Document No. 123, Copenhagen, 2008.

———, *Seeing Like a State: How Certain Schemes to Improve the Human Condition Have Failed*, London: Yale University Press, 1998.

Schmidle, Nicholas, 2009, The Saharan conundrum, *The New York Times*. February 15, 2009. http://www.nytimes.com/2009/02/15/magazine/15Africa-t.html

Security in Mobility Team, *Highlights and Key Messages*, UN-OCHA: New York, June 2010.

Seth, Sanjay, "Historical Sociology and Postcolonial Theory: Two Strategies for Challenging Eurocentrism," *International Political Sociology* Vol. 3, No. 3, 2009.

Smith, Adam, *Lectures on Jurisprudence*, R.L. Meek (ed.), Oxford: The Clarendon Press, 1978.

Sneath, David and Christopher Kaplonski, *The History of Mongolia Volume III: The Qing Period, Twentieth-century Mongolia*, Kent: Global Orient, 2010.

Sneath, David and Caroline Humphrey, *The End of Nomadism? Society, State, and the Environment in Inner Asia*, Cambridge: The White Horse Press, 2010.

Sopher, David, *The Sea Nomads: A Study Based on the Literature of the Maritime Boat People of Southeast Asia*, London: Memoirs of the National Museum, 1965.

Spivak, Gayatri, *The Spivak reader: selected works of Gayatri Chakravorty Spivak*, Donna Landry (ed.), New York: Routledge, 1996.

——— (ed.), *Selected Subaltern Studies*, New Delhi: Oxford University Press, 1988.

Sternberg, Troy, 'Unravelling Mongolia's Extreme Winter Disaster of 2010,' *Nomadic Peoples Journal*, Volume 14, Issue 1, 2010.

Stratfor Global Intelligence, "The Tuaregs: From African Nomads to Smugglers and Mercenaries," February 2, 2012. http://www.stratfor.com/analysis/tuaregs-african-nomads-smugglers-and-mercenaries

Swedish Committee for Afghanistan, "SCA receives big donation for education

REFERENCES

of Kuchi children," Accessed February 21, 2012. http://www.swedishcom-mittee.org/sca-receives-big-donation-for-education-of-kuchi-children-2

Szuchman, Jeffrey (ed.), *Nomads, Tribes, and the State in the Ancient Near East: Cross-disciplinary Perspectives*, Chicago: University of Chicago Press, 2009.

Tacitus, *Annals*, Cynthia Damon, trans., London: Penguin, 2012.

Tate, D.J.M., *The Making of Modern South-East Asia Volume I The European Conquest*, Oxford: Oxford University Press, 1977.

Thesiger, Wilfred, *Arabian Sands*, London: Penguin Classics, 2007.

Thurston, Alex, "Counterterrorism and democracy promotion in the Sahel under Presidents George W. Bush and Barack Obama from September 11, 2001, to the Nigerian Coup of February 2010" *Concerned African Scholars*. Bulletin 85, Spring 2010. Concernedafricanscholars.org

Toynbee, Arnold, *A Study of History*, Vol. III, London: Oxford University Press, 1934.

Transparency International, "Corruption Perception Index 2011," *Transparency. org*. http://cpi.transparency.org/cpi2011/results/

Turvey, Nicholas, *Rum Business: Conservation, Tourism and the Bedouin of Wadi Rum*, Oxford: Refugee Studies Centre, 2002.

UNFAO, *The State of Food Insecurity in the World*, New York: 2003. http://www.fao.org/docrep/006/

United Nations General Assembly, *United Nations Declaration on The Rights of Indigenous Peoples*, http://www.un.org/esa/socdev/unpfii/en/drip.html; Accessed August 16, 2011.

UNOCHA-PCI, '21st Century Pastoralism,' UN OCHA Pastoralist Communication Initiative: Addis Ababa, 2008.

UNODC, *World Drug Report 2009*, New York: United Nations, 2009.

UN Press Office, "COUNCIL DEMANDS SUDAN DISARM MILITIAS IN DARFUR, ADOPTING RESOLUTION 1556 (2004) BY VOTE OF 13–0–2." July 30, 2004, New York. http://www.un.org/News/Press/docs/2004/sc8160.doc.htm

Unreported World, "Meet the Janjaweed," London, Channel 4, March 14, 2008.

US Consulate, Chengdu, *Tibetan Herders In Sichuan's Hongyuan County Face Uncertain Future As County Develops*, January 11, 2010 via Wikileaks, Ref # 243033, 10CHENGDU9, http://wikileaks.org/cable/2010/01/10CHENGDU9.html

———, *Tibetan Nomad Policies In Sichuan: Settlement, Conflict And Authority*, January 8, 2010 via Wikileaks, Ref # 242869, 10CHENGDU8, http://wikileaks.org/cable/2010/01/10CHENGDU8.html

———, *Nomadic Resettlement And The New Socialist Countryside In Sichuan Provine's Aba Prefecture*, June 4, 2007 via Wikileaks, Ref # 110694, 07CHENGDU140, http://wikileaks.org/cable/2007/06/07CHENGDU140.html

REFERENCES

US Embassy, Kabul, *Afghan Human Rights Report On Kuchi-Hazara Violence: Government Inaction Could Lead To More Clashes*, February 3, 2009 via Wikileaks, Ref # 190102, 09KABUL249, http://wikileaks.org/cable/2009/02/09 KABUL249.html

——, *Director of Kuchi Directorate: Few Kuchis Will Vote, and Will Vote for Karzai*, August 16, 2009 via Wikileaks, Ref # 090KABUL2382 http://wikileaks.org/cable/2009/08/09KABUL2382.html

——, "International Human Rights Day: U.S. Embassy Brings Together Civil Society Leaders and Human Rights Activists," Press Release, December 11, 2010.

——, *Local Kuchi-Hazara Deal Dependent On National And International Actors*, June 10, 2009 via Wikileaks, Ref # 211236, "09KABUL1488" ttp://wikileaks.org/cable/2009/06/09KABUL1488.html

US Embassy, Bamako, *Observations On Unfolding Hostage Crisis In Northern Mali*, January 29, 2009 via Wikileaks Ref # 09BAMAKO63. http://wikileaks.org/cable/2009/01/09BAMAKO63.html

US Embassy, Ulaanbaatar, *Mongolia Scenesetter for Codel Boehner*, July 30, 2009 via Wikileaks, Ref # 218695, "09ULAANBAATAR208" http://www.cablegate-search.net/cable.php?id=09ULAANBAATAR208&q=mongolia

——, *Summary of High Level Meetings during Codel Boehner*. August 13, 2009 via Wikileaks, Ref # 220601, "09ULAANBAATAR236" http://www.cablegate-search.net/cable.php?id=09ULAANBAATAR236&q=mongolia

Vasilevich, G. M., and A. V. Smolyak, "Evenki," *The Peoples of Siberia*, Stephen Dunn (ed.), Chicago: The University of Chicago, 1964.

Velleman, David, "How To Share an Intention," *Philosophy and Phenomenological Research*, Vol. 57, No. 1, March 1997, pp. 29–50.

Volney, C.F., *Travels through Egypt and Syria, in the years 1783, 1784 & 1785. Containing the present natural and political state of those countries; their productions, arts, manufactures & commerce; with observations on the manners, customs and government of the Turks & Arabs*, New York: J. Tiebout, for E. Duyckinck & Co. Booksellers, 1798.

Weaver, Matthew, British hostage Edwin Dyer 'killed by al-Qaida' "Gordon Brown condemns 'barbaric' killing of Briton, who was reportedly beheaded in north Africa," *The Guardian*, June 3, 2009. http://www.guardian.co.uk/uk/2009/jun/03/edwin-dyer-hostage-killed-al-qaida?intcmp=239

Wendt, Alexander, *The Social Theory of International Politics*, Cambridge: Cambridge University Press, 2010.

Weissleder, Wolfgang, *The Nomadic Alternative: Modes and Models of Interaction in the African—Asian Deserts and Steppes*, Paris: Mouton Publisher, 1978.

Williams, Dee Mack, *Beyond Great Walls: environment, identity, and development on the Chinese grasslands of Inner Mongolia*, Stanford University Press: Stanford, 2002.

REFERENCES

WISP Staff, "How We Work," IUCN.org http://www.iucn.org/wisp/whatwisp/how_we_work/

Wolters, O.W., *Early Indonesian Commerce: A Study of the Origins of Srivijaya*, Cornell University Press, Ithaca, 1967.

World Bank, *Gross national income per capita 2010, Atlas method and PPP*, 2010. http://siteresources.worldbank.org/DATASTATISTICS/Resources/GNIPC.pdf

Young, John, *Peasant Revolution in Ethiopia: The Tigray People's Liberation Front, 1975–1991*, Cambridge University Press: Cambridge, 1997, p. 150.

Zulaika, J., "The self-fulfilling prophecies of counterterrorism", *Radical History Review*, No. 85, 2003.

INDEX

Abbala Rizeigat, 61–2
Abydos, Egypt, 22
Acheson, James M., 92
Afar Revolutionary Democratic
  Unity Front (ARDUF), 53
Afars, 52
Afghanistan, 2, 3, 17, 47, 51–6, 63,
  93, 116, 118, 119, 123
Afghanistan Independent Human
  Rights Commission, 54
African Union (AU), 64, 113
African Wildlife Foundation, 101
AFRICOM, 57
agency, 120–3
Agrawal, Arun, 69, 89–90, 107, 115
agriculture, 14–15, 23, 24, 27, 31, 52
aid, 59, 76–7, 115
AIDS (acquired immune deficiency
  syndrome), 44
Alans, 28
Alaric I, King of the Visigoths, 29
Albu Mahal, 54
Algeria, 53, 71, 72, 78–81, 112
Amerindians, 15, 67, 111, 117
anarchism, 9, 78
Andaya, Leonard, 49
Anderamboukane, Mali, 59
anthropology, 2, 3, 8, 10, 15, 21,

33–46, 48, 66, 69, 71–2, 77, 93–5,
  97, 100, 109, 116, 119, 122–3
anti-statism, 16, 17, 66, 77, 102
Anuak, 37
Aqaba, Jordan, 53
Arab Revolt (1916–18), 53
Arab Spring (2010–11), 116
Arabia, Arabs, 30, 33–6, 43, 48,
  61–5, 113
Arabian Sands (Thesiger), 91
Arctic, vii–viii, ix
Areva, 60
Ariantes, 24–5
arid environments, 91–2
The Art of Not Being Governed (Scott),
  8–14
Associated Press, 48
Auda, 36
Australia, 2, 16, 44, 82, 117
Australian Aboriginals, 44, 117
Australian Securities Exchange, 82
The Autobiography of Weni, 22
Azawad, 53, 76–7, 90, 112, 113, 118

Bagabandi, Natsagiin, 88, 89
Baghdad, Iraq, 111
Bakkarwals, 100
Baluchi, 55

161

Bamako, Mali, 58, 77, 113
Bandung Conference (1955), 17
Barfield, Thomas, 43, 93
Barrett, Richard, 57
barter economy, 69, 89–90, 107, 115
Barth, Frederick, 8, 43, 100
al-Bashir, Omar, 65
Basseri, 8, 100
Bates, Albert, 89
Bathily, Cheik Abdoulaye, 76
BBC (British Broadcasting Corporation), 105
Beard, James, 22
Bedouin, 3, 4, 8, 29–32, 34–6, 110, 117
Behsud, Wardak, 56
Berbers, 33
Berry, Wendell, 89
Bhaduri, Amit, 89
Bible, 22–4
Blemmyae, 29
Bloomberg, 108
Boehner, John, 87–8
Book of Genesis, 22–4
Booth, Ken, 7
borders, 11–13, 38–9, 50, 53, 57, 73–4, 120
Boroo Gold Mine, 108
borrow pits, 85–6
Boston Globe, 48
Bratman, Michael, 121
Brazil, 74
Bretton Woods, 17
bribery, 79, 83, 86
British East Africa (1895–1920), 99
British North Borneo Company (BNBC), 49–51
British North Borneo Herald, 49
Brunei, 81
buffalo herders, 93
Burma, 13

Burt, Robert, 45
Bury Me Standing (Fonseca), 69
Bush, George Walker, 56
Bushmen, 44
Buzan, Barry, 1, 11, 12, 50, 52

Caanan, 22–4
Cain and Abel, 22–4, 114
California, United States, 105
camels, viii, 48, 61–2, 63, 71
Canada, 16, 82, 108
Canadian First Peoples, 117
cashmere, 74
cattle, 36, 37, 52, 62, 87
Central African Republic, 61
Central Asia, ix, 4
Chad, 11–12, 61, 112
Chapel Hill University, 85
Chatty, Dawn, 5, 8, 43, 110
Chatwin, Bruce, 44–5
cheese, 87
Chengdu, Sichuan, 104
CHF International, 87
Chiang Kai-Shek, 40
China, 2, 4, 26–8, 36, 38–40, 42–3, 48, 49, 53, 71, 74, 81, 87, 91, 92, 96–9, 104, 107, 109, 114, 116, 117, 118, 119
Chingis Khan, 36
Chou, Cynthia, 116
Chou Dynasty (1046 B.C.–256 B.C.), 26
Christian Science Monitor, 93
Christianity, 22–4
Chuang, Duke of Wei, 26
civil society, 102
Clastres, Pierre, 8, 46, 122
climate change, 2, 76, 91–3, 95, 102–3, 107, 121
cocaine, 80, 112
Cold War, 17

Colombia, 80
colonialism, 8, 33, 41, 48–51, 63, 65, 72, 96
community conservation, 91
conscription, 10, 25, 50
conservation, 2, 5, 6, 7, 16, 28, 91–110, 115, 117
Constantius I, Roman Emperor, 28
Constructivism, 122
Copenhagen, Denmark, 13
copper, 81, 109
corporate social responsibility (CSR), 83, 85
corvée duties, 49
counter-insurgency, 53–4
cowboys, 111
critical theory, 13, 24, 32, 45
cyclical theory of state formation, 31, 39

Dachigam National Park, Kashmir, 95–6, 99–100, 103, 105, 109
Damascus, Syria, 31, 32, 35, 36
Dana Declaration on Mobile Peoples and Conservation (2002), 5–6, 7, 102–4, 110
Darfur, viii, 11–12, 23, 48, 53, 61–6, 67, 113, 114, 118
Darius I, King of Persia, 24, 25, 27
Davies, Jonathan, 77
Dayak, Mano, 72
Daymirdad, Wardak, 56
dehumanization, 29
Deleuze, Gilles, 45–6
Denmark, 13
Dependency Theory, 119
dervishes, 45
Desai, Lalji, 110
desertification, 97
development aid, 59, 76–7, 115
Diamond, Jared, 15

direct values, 75
discourse analysis, 3
domestic sovereignty, 11–12
droughts, viii, 66, 76, 94
drug trafficking, 58, 80–1, 112, 115
Durban, South Africa, 102
dust storms, 92
Dwyer, Michael, ix
Dyer, Edwin, 60
Dyson-Hudson, Neville, 34–5, 36

eagles, vii
Economic Community Of West African States (ECOWAS), 113
economics, 3, 4, 7, 69–90, 91, 99, 115, 116, 117
education, 52, 62, 69, 118
effective governance, 12
effective occupation, 15
Egypt, 22
emancipatory community, 7
The End of Nomadism? (Humphrey and Sneath), 3–5, 15
Enghoff, Martin, 99
Enlightenment, 32–5, 121
environment, 91–110, 119
environmental determinism, 39
Erel Mining Company, 108
Eritrea, 53–4
Ethiopia, 3, 53–4
Eurocentrism, 14, 71
Europe, 2, 17, 43, 57
Evans-Pritchard, Edward Evan, 36–8, 41
evolutionary psychology, 94
existence values, 75
existential threat to state, 47, 48–52, 115

failed states, 65, 74
al-Fasher, Sudan, viii

Feingold, Russ, 56
feudalism, 31, 41–2
Fire Nation, 108, 118
firearms, 40
Fischer, Anja, 71–2
Fisher, Eleanor, 99
Fonseca, Isabel, 69
food production, 3, 74, 114
food security, 100, 114
Forces Armées et de Sécurité du
    Mali, 111
Forster, Edward Morgan, 36
Fortune, 82
fossil isotope analysis, 31
Fox News, 48
France, viii, 22, 33, 45, 57, 60
France 24, 60
Free and Prior Informed Consent
    (FPIC), 84, 116, 118
Friedland, Robert, 85
Front Populaire de Libération de
    l'Azawad (FPLA), 76–7, 90
Fur, 63, 64
Fur Sultanate (1603–1916), 67

Galvin, Kathleen, 101
Ganya, Francis Chachu, 109–10
Gao, Mali, 58
Gashuun Sukhait, Mongolia, 87
Gellner, Ernest, 8, 41–2
Genesis, Book of 22–4
Geneva Convention, 18
genocide, 62, 64
Germany, 26, 57
gers, 84, 86, 88
Ghadames, Libya, 78
Ghazni province, Afghanistan, 51
Gilbert, Jérémie, 2, 3, 14–18
global citizens, 8
globalization, 12, 67, 71–2, 114
Glubb, John Bagot, 8

goats, 71, 87
Gobi Desert, 27, 28, 81–9, 90,
    107–9, 116, 119
gold, 81, 108
Goldman Environmental Prize, 105,
    107
Goldman Foundation, 105, 107
Goths, 29
Govind Pashu Vihar National Park,
    Uttarakhand, 104
Grasberg mine, Indonesia, 82
Greco-Persian wars, 24
Greece, 24–6
green tea, 71, 79
greenwashing, 85
Griessinger, Andreas, 122
GSPC (Groupe Salafiste pour la
    Prédication et le Combat), 58
Guardian, 102
Guattari, Félix, 45–6
Guinea, 80
gypsies, ix, 69

Hagar, Ali, 65
The Hague, Netherlands, 12
Hama Kougali, Mali, 76–7
Han Chinese, 98, 99
Han Dynasty, Western (206 B.C.–9
    A.D.), 26
Hanbogd, Mongolia, 84
Hannoum, Abdelmajid, 33
Hardin, Garrett, 91–5, 97, 116
hardpack roads, 85–6
Harris, R.B., 91, 96, 97, 98
Hatfield, Richard, 77
Hazarajat, Hazaras, 54–5, 114, 119
health services, 62, 118
Hegel, Georg Wilhelm Friedrich,
    122
Hemeti, Hamdan, 62–3, 67
Herodotus, 24–6, 28, 29, 44

Hesse, Ced, 74, 77, 96, 116
Hilal, Musa, 63–6
Hiluxes, viii
Himalayas, 93
Histoire des Berbères, 33
Hobbes, Thomas, 11, 12, 14, 19
Honneth, Axel, 122
human rights, 15, 16, 82, 86
human trafficking, 58
humanism, 15
humanitarian intervention, 54–6
Hume, David, 46
Humphrey, Caroline, 3–5, 15, 119, 123
Huns, 28–9
hunter-gatherers, 3, 10, 18

Ibn Khaldun, 30–3, 39, 43, 119
Idanthyrsus, 25, 27
ag Inaka, Sididi, 70–1
Independent Directorate of Kuchis (IDK), 53
Independent Election Commission (IEC), 56
India, 74, 89–90, 91, 93, 96, 100, 105, 110
Indigenous and Tribal Peoples Convention (1991), 6
indigenous peoples theory, 5, 6
indigenous peoples' rights, 2, 16–19, 82, 84, 115
indirect rule, 32
indirect values, 75
Indonesia, 10, 82, 116
industrialization, 40
Inner Asian Frontiers of China (Lattimore), 38
Inner Mongolia, 117, 118
insurgency, 51, 53–4
interdependence sovereignty, 11–12
International Criminal Court (ICC), 65

International Labour Organization (ILO), 6
international law, 2, 12, 15–19, 117
international legal sovereignty, 11–12
International Monetary Fund (IMF), 17
international non-governmental organizations (INGOs), 18, 77, 91, 101, 102–4, 109–10
international relations (IR), ix, 1–3, 10, 11–14, 32, 34–5, 43, 46, 81, 91, 116, 117, 120, 122
International Relations and Global Climate Change (Luterbacher and Sprinz), 92–3
International Security Assistance Force (ISAF), 56
International Union for Conservation of Nature (IUCN), 103
Iran, 8
Iraq, 53, 111
IRIN (Integrated Regional Information Networks), 55
Irons, William, 43
Isidoros, Konstantina, 58
Islam, viii, 29–30, 43, 45
Islamism, 56–60, 112
Israel, 53, 105, 117
Italy, 37, 71
Ivanhoe, 82, 85, 88

Janabi, 54
Janjaweed, 2, 16, 48, 53, 61–5, 114, 118
Japan, 71, 72
al-Jazeera, 57
Jha, Nabi, 93
John the Baptist, 45
Johore Sultanate, 10, 16, 48–51, 65
Jordan, 5, 53
Journal of Arid Environments, 91

journalism, 44, 47, 48, 63, 69, 70, 91, 116
Judaism, 105

Kabo, Vladimir 42
Kabul, Afghanistan, 53
Kalahari Bushmen, 44
Kaldor, Mary, 66–7, 115
Kant, Immanuel, 13, 14, 33
Kashmir, 95–6, 99–100, 103, 105, 109, 114
Keenan, Jeremy, 57
Kel Ahaggar, 71
Kenya, 2, 3, 12, 53, 73–5, 76, 93, 96, 102, 110, 116, 121
al-Khalil, 78–81
Khan Bank, 88
Khartoum, Sudan, 102
Khazanov, Anatoly Mikhailovich, 21, 34, 35, 42–3
Kilcullen, David, 54
Kismayo, Somalia, 114
Koran, 29–30
Krasner, Stephen, 2, 11–12, 15, 18, 115
Kuchis, 51–6, 63, 118, 119, 123
Kyoto Protocol, 93

land tenure, viii
Lapland, vii
The Later Roman Empire (Marcellinus), 28–9
Lattimore, Owen, 8, 27, 36, 38–41, 43, 44, 122
Lauvergeon, Anne, 60
Lawrence, Thomas Edward, ix, 30, 35–6
leather, 74
legibility, 39
Leica cameras, ix
Levant, 22

Leviathan (Hobbes), 19
Lewis, I.M., 43, 66
Li-Po, 45
Libya, 72, 78, 112, 116
lineage systems, 36, 38
Linklater, Andrew, 13
literacy, 52
Little, Peter, 53, 73–4, 116
Little, Richard, 1, 11, 12
livestock, vii, viii, 3, 4, 18, 36, 37, 52, 66, 71, 73–6, 78, 92, 94, 96, 98, 101, 105, 108, 115, 120
Livy, 28
Locke, John, 2, 14–15, 17, 19, 115
Loliondo, Tanzania, 101
London, England, 13
London Stock Exchange, 82
Louis-Stevenson, Robert, 45
Lucretius, 46
Luterbacher, Urs, 92–3, 102
lynx, vii

Maasalit, 63
MacGregor, James, 74, 77, 96, 116
Machiavelli, Niccolò, 32
Mali, viii, 2, 53, 57–60, 70, 72, 76, 78–81, 111–14
Malinowski, Bronisław Kasper, 35, 38
Mamdani, Mahmoud, 61–3, 65
manure, 74
Marcellinus, Ammianus, 28–9, 35
Mariette, Auguste, 22
Markov, Vladimir 42
Marx, Karl, 1
Marxism, 41
Masai Mara, 95, 99, 100–1, 114
Mashuds, 54
Massumi, Brian, 45–6
Mauritania, 57, 113
McCabe, Terrence, 93–5

McCarthy, Joseph, 40
McCay, Bonnie J., 92
McRae, Cameron, 83, 87
meat, 29, 74, 114
Mecca, Arabia, 34
media, 44, 47, 48, 63, 69, 70, 91, 116
Medina, Arabia, 30
memorandum of understanding (MOU), 62
Ménaka, Mali, 58
mercenaries, 30
Midal, Assan, 60
migration, migratory routes, 40, 79, 81
military assets, 47, 52–4, 115
milk, 74, 87
minerals, mining, 81–9, 108, 116, 118, 119, 120
Mo-tun, 27–8
mobility, 4–7, 10, 16, 23, 38, 31, 37–40, 49–53, 56, 60, 67, 69, 71–2, 74–5, 78, 90, 100, 104, 106, 112, 115, 118, 121
Moby Dick (Melville), 36
modernity, 4, 78
modernization theory, 4, 12, 14, 21, 118
Mogadishites, 66
Mohammed, Prophet of Islam, 45
Molyneux, John H., 49–51
Mongolia, Mongolians, 2, 3, 4, 28, 38, 48, 52, 81–9, 90, 91, 95, 98, 105–9, 110, 111, 114, 116, 117, 118, 119
de Montaigne, Michel Eyquem, 45
Moore, Barrington, 122
Mouvement National pour la Libération de l'Azawad (MNLA), 53, 76, 112, 113, 118
multi-national corporations (MNCs), 50, 60, 81–9, 105–9, 110, 111, 114, 120
Munkhbayar, Tsetsegee, 105–9, 110, 111, 118
Muqaddimah (Ibn Khaldun), 31, 33
music, 117

Nairobi, Kenya, 102, 121
narcotics, 58, 80–1, 112, 115
Nasser, Gamal Abdel, 17
National Committee for the Restoration of Democracy and State (CNRDR), 111–12
Native Americans, 15, 67, 111, 117
Nehru, Jawaharlal, 17
neo-liberalism, 4
New Haven, Connecticut, 13
New International Economic Order, 17
new wars, 47, 65–7, 115
New York, United States, 13, 110
New York Times, 48, 57
Ngorogoro Conservation Area (NCA), 100
Nietzsche, Friedrich Wilhelm, 46
Niger, 57
Nigeria, 112
Nile River, 22
Nimaey, Niger, 60
noble savage, 21
The Nomadic Alternative (Barfield), 43
Nomadic Lex Specialis, 2, 18
Nomadic Peoples Journal, 99
Nomadic Territories: A Human Rights Approach to Nomadic People's Land Rights (Gilbert), 14
nomads
    aid, distribution of, 59, 76–7, 115
    barter economy, 69, 89–90, 107, 115
    and conservation, environmental policy, 91–110, 119

definition of, 1–11, 115
drug trafficking, 58, 80–1, 112, 115
and economics, 3, 4, 7, 69–90, 91, 99, 115, 116, 117
etymology, 3
existential threat to state, 47, 48–52, 115
food production, security, 3, 74, 100, 114
goods, acquisition of, 30
hunter-gatherers, 3, 10, 18
livestock, vii, viii, 3, 4, 18, 36, 37, 52, 66, 71, 73–6, 78, 92, 94, 96, 98, 101, 105, 108, 115, 120
as military asset, 47, 52–4, 115
mobility, 4–7, 10, 16, 23, 38, 31, 37–40, 49–53, 56, 60, 67, 69, 71–2, 74–5, 78, 90, 100, 104, 106, 112, 115, 118, 121
new wars, 47, 65–7, 115
pastoralism, vii, viii, 3, 4, 5, 6, 10, 21, 23, 31, 33, 36, 37, 40, 42, 43, 52, 56, 66, 73–6, 89, 90, 92–110, 114, 120
racial politics, 61–5, 115
as reconciliating agents, 54–6, 115
resource competition, 54, 55, 57, 65
sea gypsies, 10, 16, 48–51, 116
security, securitization, 2, 11, 12, 14, 47–67, 91, 99, 115, 117
sedentarization, 4, 8, 12–14, 32, 39, 49–52, 53, 65–6, 89, 97, 98–9, 104, 118, 119
semi-nomads, 8
as service providers, 3
smuggling, 58, 80–1, 115
state-evasion, 8–12, 16, 17, 18, 33–4, 74, 75, 116
swidden agriculture, 10

as terrorists, 47, 54, 55, 56–60, 80, 115
trade, 2, 13, 58, 77–81, 115
transhumance, 6
violence myth, 23, 24, 28, 64
wealth, exploitation of, 39
Nomads and the Outside World (Khaza-nov), 21
Non-alignment movement, 17
non-governmental organiza-tions (NGOs), 5, 18, 60, 63, 77, 82–3, 85, 87, 91, 101, 102–4, 105, 109–10, 114, 116, 117
non-state actors, 50, 54, 93
non-state consciousness, 17
North America, 15, 111, 117; *see also* Canada, United States
North Carolina, United States, 85
Norway, vii–viii, 3, 82
Nouakchott, Mauritania, 113
Nuer, 36–7
Nunavut, 2
al-Nur, Abdelwahid, 62, 64

Obama, Barack, 56
Occidental Petroleum Company, 110
Oman, 110
Onggi River, 106, 108
Operation Enduring Freedom—Trans Sahara, 80
option value, 75
Orang Laut, 10, 16, 48–51, 116
Organization for Economic Cooper-ation and Development (OECD), 83
otherization, 29, 32, 64, 65
ag Ouefene, Sikabar, 59
overgrazing, 92–8
Oxford English Dictionary, 3
Oyu Tolgoi mine, Mongolia, 81–9
Oyun, Sanjaasuren, 108

Pakistan, 51, 53, 54, 56, 118
Palo Alto, California, 13
pan-Africanism, 112
Paris, France, 45
Pascal, Blaise, 44
Pashtuns, 51, 55, 63
Pastoral Advisory Group (PAG), 103
pastoralism, vii, viii, 3, 4, 5, 6, 10, 21, 23, 31, 33, 36, 37, 40, 42, 43, 52, 56, 66, 73–6, 89, 90, 92–110, 114, 120
Pastoralists (Salzman), 43
Peabody Energy, 88
People's Armed Police (PAP), 98
peripheral zones, 9
perpetual mobility, 7
Persia, 10, 24, 25, 27, 43
Perth, Australia, 83
Pettit, Philip, 121
piracy, 49
Pliny the Elder, 29
Polisario, 2
political economy, 70
post-colonialism, 8, 33
Potapov, Leonid Pavlovich, 42
primitive societies, 7, 11, 13, 71, 89
property, 2, 14–15, 17, 77
    cultivation, 14
    resource extraction, 14, 27, 28, 59, 69, 81–9
Proust, Marcel, 45

al-Qaeda, 56–60, 112
Qatar, 81
Qiang Prefecture, China, 107
Qinghai-Tibetan Plateau (QTP), 92, 97–9, 114, 118

racial politics, 61–5, 115
Raikas, 89–90
railways, 40

Rajasthan, 69
rangeland, 92–8
Rao, Aparna, 95–6, 99–100, 103, 105, 109
Raustiala, Kal, 103
Rawat, G.S., 93
realpolitik, 40, 55
reconciling agents, 54–6, 115
Records of The Grand Historian (Ssu-Ma), 26–8
reindeer, vii
resources, 5, 9, 13
    competition, 54, 55, 57, 65
    extraction, 14, 27, 28, 59, 69, 81–9
    nationalism, 108
responsibility to protect, 65, 114
Reuters, 48
Richard and Rhoda Goldman Fund, 105
Rio Tinto, 82–6, 88, 90, 116, 118, 119, 120
Rizegat, 11–12, 61–2
Robertson Smith, William, 34–5
Roma, 17, 30
Roman Empire (27 B.C.–395 A.D.), 28–9
Rosenberg, Justin, 1, 4
Rousseau, Jean-Jacques, 14
Ruggie, John, 122
Rūmī, Jalāl ad-Dīn Muhammad, 45
Rural Development Campaign, 66
Russia, 4; *see also* Soviet Union

Sahara Desert, 47, 56–60, 71–3, 77–8, 82, 90, 104, 112, 113, 116
Sahel region, viii, 2, 53, 56–65, 70, 72, 76, 78–81, 94, 111–14
Said, Edward, 18
Salzman, Philip Carl, 3, 43
Sami, vii–viii, 3

San Francisco, California, 105
Sanborn, John 'Black Whiskers', 111
sand-dwellers, 22, 24, 25
Sanogo, Amadou, 111
Saracens, 28
Sather, Clifford, 48, 50
Scheele, Judith, 77–81, 90, 116
Scholze, Marko, 72–3
Scotsman, The, 48
Scott, James C., 2, 8–14, 16, 18,
    33–4, 39, 44, 50, 74, 78, 116, 122
Scythians, 24–6, 29
sea gypsies, 10
Second Treatise of Government (Locke),
    14, 19
Second World War, *see* World War II
security, securitization, 2, 11, 12, 14,
    47–67, 91, 99, 115, 117
sedentarization, 4, 8, 12–14, 32, 39,
    49–52, 53, 65–6, 89, 97, 98–9,
    104, 118, 119
*The Segovia Declaration of Nomadic and
    Transhumant Pastoralists*, 6
semi-nomads, 8
Sen, Amartya, 89
Serengeti National Park, 18, 99, 100
service providers, 3
Seven Pillars of Wisdom (Lawrence), 35
Shakespeare, Nicholas, 45
sheep, 87
shifta, 111
Shiji (Ssu-Ma), 26
Shnirelman, V.A., 42
show families, 87–8
Sinai, 22
Sissoko, Django, 58
Smith, Adam, 1, 33
Smith, Steve, 11
Smugglers and Saints of the Sahara
    (Scheele), 77–81
smuggling, 58, 80–1, 115

Sneath, David, 3–5, 15, 119, 123
Social Contract, The (Rousseau), 19
social services, 52, 62
social totality, 7
Somalia, 53, 56, 66, 73–4, 111, 114,
    116
Somalia: Economy Without State (Little),
    53, 73–4
Somerset, England, 14
Songlines, The (Chatwin), 44–5
South America, 67
South China Sea, 111
Southeast Asia, 9–10, 16, 48–51, 78,
    111, 116
sovereignty, 9, 11–12, 47, 48–52
Soviet Union (1922–1991), 31, 40–3,
    66
Spinoza, Baruch, 46
Spirit of Bandung, 17
Spring and Autumn period (771
    B.C.–476 B.C.), 26
Sprinz, Detlef, 92–3
Ssu-Ma-Chi'en, 26, 44
state-centrism, 11, 13, 105, 114
state-evasion, 8–12, 16, 17, 18, 33–4,
    74, 75, 116
states
    conscription, 10, 25, 50
    failed states, 65, 74
    formation of, 31, 32
    legibility, 39
    sedentarization, 4, 8, 12, 15, 39,
        49–52, 53, 65–6, 89, 97, 98–9,
        104, 118, 119
    sovereignty, 9, 11–12, 47, 48–52
    state-centrism, 11, 13, 105, 114
    statism, 16, 65, 66, 120
    taxation, 10–11, 12, 25, 44, 50–1,
        64, 74, 75, 96
statism, 16, 65, 66, 120
steppe, 10, 26, 38, 39, 42, 95, 114,
    117

The Struggle for Recognition: The Moral Grammar of Social Conflicts (Honneth), 122
subsistence, 70
Sudan, viii, ix, 2, 3, 9, 11–12, 16, 23, 37, 47, 48, 53, 61–6, 67, 102, 112, 113, 114
Sudanese Liberation Movement (SLM), 62
Sudanese Revolutionary Front (SRF), 53
Sufism, viii, 45
Sukhbataar square, Ulaanbaatar, 83, 108
Sulemankheil, Abdul Wahab, 53–4
Suras, 29–30
Swat Valley, Pakistan, 54
swidden agriculture, 10
Switzerland, 57
Syria, 9, 31, 32, 33, 35, 36
Syrian Civil War, 116

Tacitus, 26, 28
Taghat Melet Tuareg, 59
Tajiks, 55
Taliban, 51, 53, 54, 55, 63
Tamerlane, 31, 32
Tanzania, 17, 18, 75, 76, 91, 95, 99, 100–1
taxation, 10–11, 12, 25, 44, 50–1, 64, 74, 75, 96
technology, 40, 71, 78
teleology, 32, 33, 41
terra nullius, 16, 52, 57, 60, 95
terrorism, 47, 54, 55, 56–60, 80, 115
Thesiger, Wilfred, 91, 100
Thompson, Edward Palmer, 122
A Thousand Plateaus (Massumi), 45
Tibetan Plateau, 92, 97–9, 114, 118
Tigrayan People's Liberation Front (TPLF), 47, 52

Timbuktu, Mali, 78, 112
Tin Aouker, Mali, 77
Tolstov, S.F., 41
Tolybekov, Sergali, 42
Tooze, Roger, 4
Total Economic Value (TEV), 74–5
Touat, Algeria, 79
Touré, Amadou Toumani, 58, 112
tourism, 18, 57, 72–3, 75, 99–100
Toxic Bob, 85
Toyota Land Cruisers, 72
trade, 2, 13, 58, 77–81, 115
Tragedy of the Commons, The (Hardin), 91–5, 97, 114, 116
transhumance, 6
Transparency International, 106–7
Tuareg, viii, 2, 53, 54, 57–60, 70, 72–3, 76–81, 90, 104, 112–13, 117
Turkey, 53
Turkmen, 55
Tydings Committee, 40

Uganda, 53, 75, 76, 102
Ulaanbaatar, Mongolia, 83, 85, 108
United Kingdom (UK), 13, 14, 49–51, 57, 59, 82
United Nations (UN), viii, 16, 17, 48, 57, 61, 63, 64, 76, 80, 81, 84, 102, 114, 118, 119, 120
Declaration on the Rights of Indigenous Peoples (UNDRIP), 17, 84
Environment Programme (UNEP), 120
Office for the Coordination of Humanitarian Affairs, 63
Office of Drugs and Crime (UNODC), 80
Security Council, 61
World Food Program (WFP), 76–7

United States (US), 2, 13, 15, 51–2,
54–9, 64, 80, 87–8, 96, 98, 99,
104, 105, 110, 111, 113, 117, 118,
119, 120, 121, 123
Agency for International Development (USAID), 87–8
Counter-Insurgency Handbook,
54
Office of War Information, 40
University of Wisconsin, 42
uranium, 59
urbanization, 31, 66, 118
USA Today, 48
Uttarakhand, India, 93, 104

Valens, Roman Emperor, 28
Van Gujjars, 93, 104–5
de Vattel, Emer, 14
Velleman, David, 121
Vidal, John, 102
violence, 23, 24, 28, 64, 67, 74,
110–11, 118
Visigoths, 29
Vladimirtsov, Boris, 42
Volney, Constantin François, 33–4,
119
de Waal, Alex, viii, 53, 61, 63–4

Wadi Dana Nature, Jordan, 5
Waever, Ole, 50, 52
war on terror, 56
Wardak province, Afghanistan, 51
Washington Post, 70
water supplies, 62
Watson, Burton, 26, 27
Waziristan, 51

Wazirs, 54
wealth, exploitation of, 39
Wendt, Alexander, 122
Weni, 22, 25
Westphalian sovereignty, 11–12
Whitman, Walter, 45
Wikileaks, 120
de Wilde, Jaap, 50
Wildlife Institute of India, 93
World Alliance of Mobile Indig-
enous Peoples (WAMIP), 102,
109–10, 116, 120
World Food Program (WFP), 76–7
World Initiative for Sustainable
Pastoralism (WISP), 103
World War II (1939–45), 9, 37, 40
World Wildlife Fund, 101
Wu, Emperor of the Western Han
Dynasty, 26

Xiongnu, 26–8

Yale University, 13
Yangtze River, 92
Yellow River, 92
Yemen, 53, 56
Yomuts, 10, 43
ag Youssef, Ibrahim, viii, 76, 78, 104,
112, 113
Yugoslavia, 83
yurts, 84, 86, 88

Zafzaf, Hammu, 79
Zaghawa, 63
Zigong, Sichuan, 99
Zorig Foundation, 83